DAVID M. JONES

THE
BUCK
STARTS
HERE

HOW THE
FEDERAL RESERVE CAN
MAKE OR BREAK
YOUR FINANCIAL FUTURE

PRENTICE HALL
Englewood Cliffs, New Jersey 07632

Prentice-Hall International (UK) Limited, *London*
Prentice-Hall of Australia Pty. Limited, *Sydney*
Prentice-Hall Canada, Inc., *Toronto*
Prentice-Hall Hispanoamericana, S.A., *Mexico*
Prentice-Hall of India Private Limited, *New Delhi*
Prentice-Hall of Japan, Inc., *Tokyo*
Simon & Schuster Asia Pte. Ltd., *Singapore*
Editora Prentice-Hall do Brasil, Ltda., *Rio de Janeiro*

© 1995 by

Prentice Hall

10   9   8   7   6   5   4   3   2   1

Library of Congress Cataloging-in-Publication Data

Jones, David M. (David Milton)
    The buck starts here : how the Federal Reserve can make or break
your financial future / a book by David M. Jones.
        p.   cm.
    Includes bibliographical references and index.
    ISBN 0–13–180498–7
    1. Investments—United States.   2. Securities—United States.
3. Monetary policy—United States.   4. Fiscal policy—United States.
I. Title.
HG4910.J66   1995
332.1'1'0973—dc20   94–38365
                                                                 CIP

ISBN 0-13-180498-7

PRENTICE HALL
Career & Personal Development
Englewood Cliffs, New Jersey 07632

Simon & Schuster, A Paramount Communication Company

Printed in the United States of America

This book is dedicated to my wife, Becky, and our children David, Jennifer, and Stephen, who give meaning to all that I do through their love, family unity, and untiring support.

ACKNOWLEDGMENTS

*F*or sharing their knowledge and experience in monetary policy, I express my deepest appreciation to Alan Greenspan, chairman of the Federal Reserve Board of Governors; David Mullins, former vice chairman of the Federal Reserve Board of Governors; Edward (Mike) Kelley, member, Federal Reserve Board of Governors; Joe Coyne, assistant to the Federal Reserve Board of Governors; and Mike Prell, director of research, Federal Reserve Board of Governors. Also, for general information on banking and equity market research, my thanks go to my friend Carter Bacot, chairman of the Bank of New York. For insights on foreign exchange, I thank another good friend, Geoffrey Bell, of Geoffrey Bell & Associates.

For their perspectives on personal finance topics and the media I want to give special thanks to PBS's Robert MacNeil and Jim Lehrer of the "MacNeil Lehrer NewsHour"; Jerry Goodman, host of "Adam Smith's Moneyworld"; and Paul Kangas and Cassie Seifert of the "Nightly Business Report"; CNN's Lou Dobbs, Bill Hartley, Myron Kandel, Jan Hopkins, Stuart Varney, and Deborah Marchini; Ken and Daria Dolan of WOR Radio; and Ray Brady of the "CBS Evening News." Others to whom I owe special recognition are Charles Gibson and Joan Lunden of ABC's "Good Morning America"; Consuelo Mack of "The Wall Street Journal Report"; and Dean Sheppard, Sue Herera, Bill Griffith, Ron Insana, and Neil Cavuto of CNBC.

Last, but by no means least, I want to offer heartfelt gratitude to my colleagues at Aubrey G. Lanston & Co., Inc., without whom this project would never have been possible. My trusted associate Bob Falconer's comments on the manuscript of this book were invaluable. Indispensable assistance was also provided by Wilson Lam, Patricia Thrapp, Lee Youngdahl, Todd Speiser, Jim Mirenda, and Alan Danneels. Special thanks are due to my irreplaceable secretary and administrative assistant, Margaret Kormanik, for her preparation of the manuscript and to Lisa Zindorf who designed all my exhibits, tables, and charts. Gratitude goes also to my exceptional editor, Caroline Carney, who encouraged me to start this project and kept me on track with her many writing and communication skills and special insights.

CONTENTS

FIGURES, EXHIBITS, AND TABLES

FIGURES

EXHIBITS

TABLES

PREFACE

This book is intended for everyone who has been lucky enough to build a nest egg out of many hard-earned paychecks, and who wants to see it appreciate rather than decline in value. If you're like most people, you treasure your savings and investments because you see them as your ticket to financial independence. For this reason you want to protect your cash, mutual funds, stocks, bonds, real estate, or other personal assets from any adversity in the financial markets or the economy. The only way to do this with a consistent degree of success is to become an astute observer of Federal Reserve policy shifts.

The Fed is the most important and effective government policymaking body. Its impact on the financial markets is unparalleled. The most recent vivid demonstration of the Fed's impact on the stock and bond markets came on Friday, February 4, 1994, when the Fed tightened up on the supply of credit for the first time in five years. Shockingly, stock prices fell 96 points on that day alone. On March 22, the Fed tightened a second time. By April 4, the Dow-Jones Industrial Average had plunged 10%, and the yield on 30-year Treasury bonds had surged to 7.43% from 6.23% at the end of January 1994. This shocking surge in yields was associated with a 14% decline in the price of 30-year Treasury bonds, the steepest two-month decline since 1980. The Fed tightened a third time on April 18, 1994. In early May, the 30-year Treasury bond yield touched 7.64%. On May 17, the Fed tightened a fourth time (by twice as much) and, in contrast with its earlier tightening steps, attempted to explain what it was doing. In response, both bonds and stocks initially staged a strong rally. Just the same, during the first six months of 1994, stock mutual funds suffered a 5.5% decline in total return while bond mutual funds dropped about 2.7%. After no change in its policy stance at its meeting on July 5–6, the Fed tightened a fifth time on August 16, 1994.

Of course, it is important to note that this stock and bond market slump reflected not only the Fed's tightening moves, but also an unexpected surge in economic growth and hints of future inflation. Additional factors were unexpected trade problems with Japan, political instability caused by the Whitewater scandal, technical problems in the mortgage securities market, and volatility in the global markets. But from your own perspective, the harsh reality is that after a spectacular year in 1993, the Fed's actions to depress credit have driven your stock and bond returns sharply lower in the first half of 1994.

However, you do not have to sit by helplessly watching your hard-earned investments evaporate. Using Fed policy shifts as the key to making major adjustments among your holdings of money, bonds, equities, and other investments will help you maintain a good balance between risk and reward while simultaneously achieving the twin objectives of enhancing the value of your asset holdings in good times and preserving it in bad times. Truly, "the buck starts here," as the large plaque on current Fed Chairman Alan Greenspan's desk proclaims.

By now, you might be convinced that keeping an eye on the Fed is the best defense: it's also a very strong offense. *The Buck Starts Here* will help you understand and perhaps even anticipate the actions of the Fed and turn this information into extra profits on your investments. For example, you'll learn that when the Fed is easing, or increasing, the availability of credit, interest rates on short-term money market investments such as Treasury bills and bank CDs will decline immediately, and bond yields will eventually follow suit. That's your signal to turn toward long-term bonds and stocks as relatively more attractive investment vehicles for your balanced portfolio. That's just one example of the many ways that you can use knowledge of the Fed to enrich your returns.

This book will show you many ways to make the Fed a partner in your investment success. It starts with a discussion of how you can make sense out of your economic environment and use this knowledge to your advantage in managing your asset holdings. It will reveal which economic developments are important and which are not, and how to identify cyclical ups and downs with the "sacred seven" indicators, selected especially for you. This book will examine why our latest "balance sheet" recession and recovery is different from past ones and what it means for the profitability of your investment holdings. Also, there is an analysis of the importance of inflationary psychology in your choice of investments.

Next, we'll take an inside look at Washington's politics and power, and most important, we'll find out how the government affects your investment performance. We'll analyze how Federal budget discipline can affect your bond investing success. We'll also come up with new clues that signal future Fed policy shifts. You can use these clues to anticipate shifts in Fed policy so that, in turn, you can make timely shifts among money market investments, bonds, stocks, and other assets in your portfolio. You also will learn how the relationship between Fed Chairman Alan Greenspan and the Clinton administration might affect your financial fortunes.

Then we show exactly how you stand to benefit from the spectacular democratization of the capital markets. Today's individual investor can choose from a vast array of investment opportunities. We'll show you how to evaluate those choices. Also, we'll take a look at the impact of exchange rate fluctuations on the value of your holdings of global securities, and we'll forecast whether bank CDs will regain their luster. In addition, we'll face up to the jarring reality that your "diversified portfolio" holding both U.S. and foreign stocks and bonds is more susceptible to market shocks than you think, and we'll show you how to respond to this situation.

The book closes with a step-by-step guide to keeping pace with the Fed and the economy. You will discover how you can profit from the explosion in mutual fund choices, and you will find out how to create a balanced portfolio with a favorable-risk-return trade-off that allows you to sleep more peacefully and prosperously each night.

CARVING A PROSPEROUS PATH THROUGH THE INVESTMENT JUNGLE

*I*nvesting intelligently can be as exhilarating as sailing the open seas if you are in harmony with the elements and on a profitable tack. But just as your course can be disrupted by gale winds or hidden shoals, your investment goals can cause you to capsize if you don't take certain precautions. The most important of these is becoming a more savvy observer of the Federal Reserve. This book offers you a simple system keyed on the Federal Reserve that will heighten your returns and also alert you to any unforseen danger lying ahead.

For nearly all bond and stock market investors, the year 1993 may be about as close to heaven as you will get, at least in this lifetime. The Federal Reserve was willingly pumping new credit into the system, interest rates were declining, the economy was on the right course, and no one expected inflation to rear its ugly head anytime soon. This was a near-perfect environment for rallies in both the stock and bond markets. And the Dow-Jones Industrial Average responded by soaring to a 17% gain in total return (price appreciation plus dividends).

Absolutely essential to your investment success in 1993 in the stock and bond markets was the Federal Reserve's benevolence. The Fed is a sort of bankers' bank or central bank that has a huge impact on your investment fortunes. The Fed is the only institution capable of creating money out of thin air. When the Fed is pumping new funds into the economy and lowering the cost of borrowing (interest rates), you can almost always expect big rallies in bonds and stocks.

The chairman of the Federal Reserve Board of Governors (currently Alan Greenspan) is arguably the second most important person in our government, next to the president. The chairman and the vice chairman of the Federal Reserve Board of Governors are appointed by the president to four-year terms (renewable at the president's pleasure), with the advice and consent of the Senate.

To expand money and credit growth and push short-term interest rates lower, the Fed buys U.S. government securities, thereby adding to bank reserves. This increase in bank reserves supports an expansion in bank credit (loans and investments) and deposits and, in turn, stimulates economic activity—usually with a time lag of 6 to 12 months. Alternatively, to restrain money and credit growth and push short-term interest rates higher, the Fed sells U.S. government securities, thereby contracting bank reserves. Those actions depress economic activity, usually with a time lag of 3 to 9 months. As a rule, the Fed is more effective in restraining economic growth than in stimulating it. Regarding the latter, there is an old saying that the Fed can drive a horse to water but it can't make the horse drink.

The federal funds rate is the Fed's main policy instrument. It is the rate on bank reserve balances at the Fed that are loaned and borrowed among banks, usually overnight. When the Fed tightens the availability of credit, it pushes the federal funds rate higher. Conversely, when the Fed expands the supply of credit, it pushes the federal funds rate lower.

The Fed's actions to expand the supply of credit during the period from June 1989 through September 1992 pushed short-term rates down more sharply than long-term rates, thereby making bond investments attractive. An improving bond market, in turn, gave stocks a boost. Bank earnings surged as the decline in the short-term interest rates banks pay for funds far exceeded the drop in the longer-term interest rates that banks earn on their loans and investments (credit). At the same time, against the background of declining interest rates, individuals and businesses were able to refinance their heavy debt positions, thereby reducing the burden of interest and principal payments. Taken together, these Fed easing actions, combined with the taxpayer bailout of failing thrift institutions, lessened the depth of the 1990–91 recession and helped strengthen the financial foundations for our current recovery.

Faced with the 1991 Fed-induced plunge in short-term interest rates, all investors suffered a sharp drop in earnings on their bank CDs and other low yielding short-term investments. To make things worse, there was also a plunge in prices of real estate and other real assets during the 1990–91 recession. In this environment, you probably were forced, especially in late 1991 and early 1992, to shift your money into higher yielding financial assets such as bond or stock mutual funds. You might have been lured into these new investments by the promises of higher returns trumpeted by a host of brokers, investment advisors, insurance agents, or even your local bankers. Your new investments might even have made good on those promises.

If you were in the financial markets, you had all-time bragging rights to your friends on how brilliantly your investment choices in mutual funds and other financial assets performed in 1993. But if you had heavy exposure in stocks and bonds, you also faced more risk than you realized as you approached the end of that highly successful year. Just around the corner, on February 4, 1994, the Fed suddenly tightened its hold on the credit reins. In response, the bond and equity markets shuddered. Stock prices fell sharply, bond yields surged, and you stopped patting yourself on the back. On the heels of the Fed's surprise tightening move, you may have joined other worried individual investors as they began to pull money out of their bond mutual funds, and move it into safer and more liquid short-term money market investments.

But it didn't stop there. Subsequently, on March 22, April 18, and May 17, the Fed followed with additional efforts to clamp down on the availability of credit. Short-term interest rates spurted higher, further unsettling the financial markets and giving you more sleepless nights as you tallied up the losses in your stock and bond mutual funds for the first half of 1994. Fed Chairman Alan Greenspan provided most of the rationale for these Fed tightening moves and likely similar future steps. In congressional testimony before the Joint Economic Committee on January 31, 1994, Greenspan noted that "the foundations of economic expansion are looking increasingly well entrenched" and warned that "monetary policy must not overstay accommodation." The reasoning of the Fed chairman and his fellow policymakers was that by acting promptly with a series of preemptive strikes against inflation, the Fed hoped to convince investors that it meant business in seeking to limit any future acceleration in inflation. It was hoped that these moderate preemptive strikes would be sufficient to keep inflationary expectations in check, thereby limiting increases in long-term interest rates.

After their decisive tightening actions on May 17, increasing both the federal funds rate and the discount rate, Fed officials seemed to imply that they had achieved their initial objective and thus might pause, at least for a short while. Specifically, the monetary authorities noted that this latest tightening step, combined with the three earlier ones, "had substantially removed the degree of monetary accommodation." For investors in bonds and stocks, this monetary policy jargon means, in essence, that the party is over. The Fed is intent on tightening its grip on the credit reins and pushing interest rates higher, boding ill for the bond and stock markets. The Fed tightened credit again on August 16, 1994.

For the past 25 years, I have been a close watcher of the Federal Reserve and its impact on the financial markets. After years of observation, I am no longer caught off guard by Fed policy shifts. I've learned how to interpret the thinking and actions of Fed officials. I track the same economic indicators and early signals of future price pressures that Fed policymakers follow. And I follow closely the "politics" between the White House, Congress, and the Fed, especially during periods when the Fed's unpopular constriction of the credit supply and raising of interest rates coincides with election time. As a consequence, I've been able to accurately forecast Fed policy shifts and the concomitant turbulence in the financial markets.

For your well-being as an investor, you too must be able to foresee and understand Fed policy shifts. If you follow the simple signals offered in this book, not only will you not be caught unaware by changes in monetary policy, but you will also increase your investment returns, reduce risk, and protect your portfolio from unforseen interest rate shocks. However, to achieve strong investment returns *and* peace of mind, you will need to make some key Fed related shifts in your money, bond, and stock holdings on an ongoing basis.

Shifting your investments in concert with the Fed's stance, though, is a refinement of your overall portfolio strategy. To start with, you need an objective, and then your watchwords for investing should be balance and diversity. In terms of portfolio balance, if you have a stomach for only moderate risk and a medium-term investment horizon, you might split your investment portfolio roughly equally between stocks and bonds. You should think of the fixed-income portion of your portfolio as a sort of security blanket. Alternatively, if you are not afraid of risk and have a long-term investment horizon, you might favor a somewhat riskier investment portfolio with potentially higher returns consisting of 75% stocks and 25% bonds. But if you happen to have little stomach for risk and a relatively short-term investment horizon, you might favor a split of 25% stocks and 75% bonds.

For diversity you look for stocks whose prices, dividends, and source of earnings are not linked to other stocks you are holding. For example, after diversifying by industry, you might spread out your equity holdings among companies of different sizes in terms of capitalization (small-cap, mid-cap, or big-cap stocks), or you might diversify your equity holdings among U.S. and foreign stocks. Within the foreign stock category, there is, of course, the basic choice between emerging markets and developed markets. The hope is that returns on these different categories of equity holdings will move independently of each other. Unfortunately, this effort at diversification is sometimes difficult to achieve, especially in extremely volatile periods when U.S. and foreign stocks and bonds tend to move together. In more normal conditions, however, some element of diversity is achievable in portfolios consisting of U.S. stocks and bonds and foreign stocks and bonds.

Still, you can't get away from the jarring reality that the Fed is the main key to your investment success (or failure). The blunt truth is that U.S. bonds and stocks and foreign bonds and stocks all beat a hasty retreat on the heels of the Fed's February 4, 1994, action to cut back on the availability of credit and to make it more costly by increasing interest rates. By keeping an eye on the Fed, you can make timely and appropriate portfolio adjustments that improve your investment returns and reduce your risk.

Section One

THE ECONOMIC EVENTS THAT DRIVE RETURNS

*T*he most successful investors pay attention only to the major economic events that bear directly on the successful management of their asset holdings. You too should look primarily for economic evidence signaling cyclical turning points—upward as recession gives way to recovery or downward as recovery gives way to recession. These cyclical turning points provide an important clue to future Federal Reserve policy actions. Consider also what has made this cycle different from its predecessors. For example, our current recovery was restrained in its early stages by "balance sheet" problems as consumers and businesses remained cautious and kept spending in check in order to ease their heavy debt taken on in the 1980s.

You can use the "sacred seven" economic indicators to pinpoint cyclical turning points. The "sacred seven" is a hand-picked group of indicators that I developed as a system for capturing the actual behavior of individuals and businesses at moments when the economy is changing direction. Included in the "sacred seven" indicators are durable goods orders, supplier deliveries, industrial production, nonfarm payrolls, motor vehicle sales, housing starts, and commodity prices.

You also might not want to overlook certain practical, personal indicators that shed light on the state of the economy. For example, to help identify a silent, grass-roots credit crunch of the type that contributed importantly to the 1990–91 recession, you might take your own informal survey of local builders and developers. In the 1990–91 experience, they were among the first to have their credit supply cut off by local bankers.

Other important, local sources of information about economic vitality can include taxi drivers, real estate agents, or retail sales clerks you meet in your home town or in your travels around the nation. You might ask questions about the level of business activity compared to previous seasons. Unquestionably, declining discretionary spending on travel for conventions and vacations can be important early indicators of darkening business and consumer sentiment. Of course, you should keep in mind that economic activity may vary widely from one region of the country to another. For example, the recent regional disparity in economic activity has been magnified by a massive cutback in defense outlays that has hit areas like California particularly hard.

In your effort to use knowledge about the economic environment to improve your investment performance, you should also consider inflation expectations; specifically, what investors, consumers, businesses, and workers believe prices for things they need will do in the future. As a rule, financial assets such as stocks and bonds will flourish during periods when the rate of increase in prices you pay for goods and services (measured by the consumer price index) is falling and when your expectation is that this trend toward diminishing inflation will continue in the future. Conversely, it is likely that increasing price pressures and rising inflationary expectations will lead to bear markets for bonds and stocks.

1

How This Economic Recovery Differs and What It Means for Your Investments

No investor can ignore economic developments. At the same time, not all economic developments are of equal importance to your finances. This chapter will reveal which economic events foretell key turning points in the financial markets. You need to watch closely for these turning points because they give you the first clue to what the Fed will do. And what the Fed does, in turn, has a critical bearing on whether you are a happy or sad investor.

FORECASTING FUTILITY

Forecasting economic activity is extremely hazardous. There's an old saying that economists were created to make weather forecasters look good. It's difficult enough to accurately forecast fundamental economic fluctuations in areas like income and spending. But it borders on the impossible to foresee important outside disturbances such as the oil price shocks of the 1970s, the Vietnam war of the 1960s, the Korean war of the 1950s, or even World War II of the 1940s.

As a smart investor, though, you don't have to have perfect foresight. Rather, train your attention on spotting those economic patterns that indicate cyclical turning points. To determine turning points, follow the movement of a few significant economic indicators. A cyclical turning point could be indicated when, for example, a majority of these economic indicators begin to diverge from a previous strengthening trend and then eventually reverse course and

Table 1.1   **Business Cycle Expansions and Contractions, 1900–1991**

Business Cycle Reference Dates		Duration (in Months)	
Trough	Peak	Contraction (Trough from Previous Peak)	Expansion (Trough to Peak)
December 1900	September 1902	18	21
August 1904	May 1907	23	33
June 1908	January 1910	13	19
January 1912	January 1913	24	12
December 1914	August 1918	23	44
March 1919	January 1920	7	10
July 1921	May 1923	18	22
July 1924	October 1926	14	27
November 1928	August 1929	13	21
March 1933	May 1937	43	50
June 1938	February 1945	13	80
October 1945	November 1948	8	37
October 1949	July 1953	11	45
May 1954	August 1957	10	39
April 1958	April 1960	8	24
February 1961	December 1969	10	106
November 1970	November 1973	11	36
March 1975	January 1980	16	58
July 1980	July 1981	6	12
November 1982	July 1990	16	92
March 1991		8	. . .

Source: National Bureau of Economic Research, Inc.

turn down. After the downturn has begun, these economic signals will again move together in a self-reinforcing way, this time in a downward direction. (For a list of cyclical turning points since 1900 see Table 1.1.)

"SACRED SEVEN"

To identify economic turning points that might have a direct impact on your investment fortunes, the first step is to pay close attention to the following, specially selected "sacred seven" economic signals: (1) supplier deliveries, (2) durable goods orders, (3) industrial production, (4) payroll employment, (5) motor vehicle sales, (6) housing starts, and (7) industrial commodity prices. Here's a quick overview of each one of the "sacred seven":

- *Nonfarm payrolls* are released on the first Friday of each month from the U.S. Bureau of Labor Statistics and are closely followed by Wall Street. Accordingly, this employment figure has the power to dramatically move the bond market, as happened recently on Good Friday (April 1, 1994). An unexpectedly large March increase in nonfarm payrolls convinced investors that the economy was rebounding strongly from weather-depressed conditions. Expecting that this rebound could eventually trigger renewed inflationary pressures, in just one day investors pushed the yield on 30-year Treasury bonds sharply higher to 7.26% from 7.08%. Needless to say, this meant hefty capital losses in your bond funds.

- *Supplier deliveries* are arguably one of the most important components of the "sacred seven." This series is, in turn, a component of the National Association of Purchasing Management (NAPM) monthly survey covering some 360 corporate purchasing managers and is published around the first of each month. Supplier delivery lead times represent the length of time between when corporate purchasing managers place their orders with suppliers and when these suppliers actually can fill those orders. Obviously, barring an earthquake or some other natural disaster, the longer the time it takes for suppliers to fill the order, the greater the inflow of orders received and the stronger the economy. Conversely, a shortening in supplier delivery lead times reflects weakening orders and a slumping economy.

- *Durable goods orders* are perhaps the most important leading indicator of cyclical turning points. These data, published around the 20th of each month by the U.S. Commerce Department, represent new orders received by manufacturers of durable goods (those goods lasting three years or more, including motor vehicles, appliances, and business machinery). In the past, unfilled orders, measured as the level of orders less shipments, represented a particularly good indicator of economic upturns (or downturns). However, with the advent of the information revolution and tight computer control of business orders, shipments, and inventories, the importance of unfilled orders in identifying cyclical ups and downs has diminished.

- *Industrial production*, measuring the output of factories, utilities and mines, is an important indicator of cyclical turning points and is published by the Federal Reserve around the

15th of each month. Cyclical upturns occur when business inventories are inadequate to meet a sudden surge in demand. In such circumstances, businesses will seek to replenish their depleted inventory stocks by placing new orders with suppliers; this, in turn, results in increasing production, employment, and income. Conversely, when inventories build up involuntarily in the face of an unexpected weakening in sales, businesses will reduce new orders, which in turn will result in declining production, employment and income.

- *Motor vehicle sales* are always an important signal that the economy may be approaching key turning points. These data are published around the 5th of each month by the auto companies. Consumer spending on goods (including motor vehicles) and services accounts for about two-thirds of total GDP. Moreover, consumer spending on motor vehicles (autos and light trucks) and other durable goods tends to be strong when consumer confidence and income growth is high. Accordingly, strong monthly increases in motor vehicle sales are likely to point toward rapid economic growth and accelerating inflationary pressures, conditions that will trigger countering Fed-tightening actions.

- *Housing starts* are published around the 15th of each month by the Commerce Department. The housing starts figure is composed of starts of single-family units and multifamily units. As an investor, you can expect that housing starts will be early indicators of cyclical upturns and downturns. These housing starts are highly sensitive to fluctuations in interest rates. Specifically, when interest rates fall to low levels, housing starts will rise; conversely, when interest rates climb to high levels, housing activity will weaken. Fed officials watch housing activity closely as one of the first sectors in our economy that responds to Fed policy shifts. Remember that as an investor seeking to anticipate Fed policy shifts, you should be watching what the Fed watches. For example, when the Fed is easing its stance with a view to increasing the availability of credit and pushing interest rates lower, the Fed will watch closely for signs of life in housing activity. In contrast, when the Fed is tightening up on the supply of credit and pushing interest rates higher, the monetary authorities will watch for signs of weakening in housing activity.

- *Commodity prices,* including the *Journal of Commerce* (JOC) index of industrial commodity prices, such as oil, steel scrap, copper, lumber, and cotton, and the Commodities Research Bureau (CRB) index of both industrial and agricultural commodities prices are important indicators of future price pressures. The JOC index is reported daily. Industrial commodities prices are especially sensitive to demand pressures. Rising prices of raw materials and other commodities in the early stages of the production pipeline will, if persistent, eventually be reflected in increases in producer prices of finished goods and consumer prices. The crude goods component of the producer price index published by the U.S. Bureau of Labor Statistics around the 12th of each month is also a good indicator of prices of commodities or raw materials as they enter the production process.

When you find, as a result of reading the daily *Wall Street Journal,* that a majority of these "sacred seven" indicators change direction, you are probably looking at a cyclical turning point in the economy. See Exhibit 1.1 for a typical monthly calendar of release dates for the sacred seven (written in bold) and other data.

If at first you have difficulty recognizing these cyclical turning points before they happen, do not give up. Even the most sophisticated and highly trained analysts find this task challenging. However, if you make even a moderate effort to analyze and track the "sacred seven," you will be rewarded with the ability to handle your investments more wisely and profitably.

Now that you understand the predictive powers of the "sacred seven," you are probably asking, "How can I put them to use right away?" The best idea is to look at these important economic signals more closely by using six simple analytical tricks. For example, you could examine the *direction* and *magnitude* of changes in these "sacred seven" economic signals (see accompanying worksheet). Also, you could look for a pattern of *consistent monthly revisions* in these economic indicators. Obviously, upturns are indicated by consistent upward revisions in the estimates of these indicators and downturns by consistent downward revisions. In addition, you could try to see if there are any signs of *self-reinforcing behavior* among these indicators. Finally, as you approach the upper stages of an economic advance you might look for *shortages* in skilled labor and *bottlenecks* in production.

Exhibit 1.1

Aubrey G. Lanston & Co. Inc.

LOOKING AHEAD: DECEMBER 1994

M	T	W	T	F
			1 AM Chain store sales, Nov 8:30 Personal inc & PCE, Oct 8:30 Merchandise trade, 3Q 10:00 Construction spending, Oct **10:00 Purchasing mgrs, Nov**	**2** **8:30 Employment, Nov** 8:30 Leading indictors, Oct 10:00 SLMA announcement 10:00 FNMA announcement 10:00 Factory orders, Oct 2:30 52 wk bill announcement
5 10:00 New home sales, Oct **Noon Auto sales, Nov** 1:30 SLMA pricing	**6** 1:30 FNMA pricing 3:00 Treasury "STRIPS' data	**7** 10:00 Productivity & costs, 3Q 10:00 SLMA announcement Noon Fed's "Tan" book released 3:00 Consumer credit, Oct	**8** 10:00 Wholesale trade, Oct 1:00 52 week bill auction 1:30 SLMA pricing	**9** 10:00 Mich sentiment, early Dec 10:00 FFCB announcement
12	**13** **8:30 Producer price index, Nov** 8:30 Retail sales, Nov 1:30 FHLMC pricing	**14** 8:30 Consumer price index, Nov **9:15 Industrial production, Nov**	**15** 10:00 Business inventories, Oct 10:00 Philadelphia Fed survey, Dec	**16** **8:30 Housing starts, Nov** 10:00 FFCB announcement
19 10:00 FHLB announcement	**20** 8:30 Trade balance, Oct 1:30 FHLB pricing FOMC meeting	**21** 8:30 Capital spending, 3Q 2:00 Treasury budget, Nov 1:30 FFCB pricing 2:30 2&5 yr note announcement	**22** 8:30 GDP, 3Q final	**23** **8:30 Durable gds orders, Nov** 8:30 Personal inc & PCE, Nov 10:00 Mich sentiment, Dec 4:30 FOMC minutes, Nov 15
26 **Christmas Day holiday observed**	**27** 8:45 Existing home sales, Nov 10:00 Consumer confidence, Dec	**28** 1:00 2 year note auction	**29** 8:30 Leading indicators, Nov 10:00 Import/export prices, Nov 1:00 5 year note auction	**30** 10:00 New home sales, Nov 10:00 Chicago purch mgrs, Dec 2:30 52 wk bill announcement 3:00 Agricultural prices, Dec

8

"SACRED SEVEN" WORKSHEET

1. Collect monthly data on the "sacred seven." To do this, you should become familiar with the accompanying calendar for monthly release dates for each item in the "sacred seven." Specifically, durable goods orders are released around the 20th of each month, supplier delivery lead times around the 1st, industrial production around the 15th, nonfarm payrolls on the first Friday, motor vehicles around the 5th, housing starts around the 15th, and producer prices of crude goods around the 12th. The JOC commodity price index is reported daily. (All these data are published in *The Wall Street Journal*.)

2. Direction of change of each indicator in latest month.

Up	Down

3. Magnitude (percentage change) in each "sacred seven" item arranged from largest to smallest. It is especially significant to take a close look at which of the "sacred seven" are showing the largest percentage increase. For example, if the economy appears to be moving from recession to recovery, and the majority of the "sacred seven" are in the "up" column and they also show the largest percentage changes, you can be more confident that a cyclical upturn is indeed at hand. Conversely, the same holds in the case of an economic downturn when the majority of the "sacred seven" indicators in the "down" column also show the largest percentage changes.

Magnitude

1. _____

2. _____

3. _____

4. _____

5. _____

6. _____

7. _____

4. Record the direction of monthly revisions in each of two preceding months available in past issues of *The Wall Street Journal* or *Barron's*. If the majority of the "sacred seven" are revised upwards, recovery is indicated. Conversely, if the majority of "sacred seven" indicators are revised downward, a weakening in the economy is indicated.

	1 Month Ago		2 Months Ago	
	Up	Down	Up	Down
Durable goods orders				
Supplier deliveries				
Industrial production				
Nonfarm payrolls				
Motor vehicle sales				
Housing starts				
Crude producer prices				

5. To help determine the sustainability of an economic recovery, put a checkmark in the appropriate column indicating the direction of change in each of the following key components of the "sacred seven" in each of the last six months.

	Preceding Month										
	1		2		3		4		5		6	
	Up	Down	Up	Down	Up	Down	Up	Down	Up	Down	Up	Down
Durable goods orders												
Industrial production												
Nonfarm payrolls												

6. Look at the number of industries indicated as operating near full capacity in Federal Reserve's beige book. If it is six or more key industries (steel, autos, auto parts, building materials, capital goods, paper, etc.), watch out, you may be moving into the advanced stages of recovery where high and rising capacity utilization rates begin to produce increasing price pressures.

7. Once you have identified a cyclical upturn (or downturn), you then want to watch the Fed's reaction to these cyclical turning points very closely. For example, when a cyclical upturn advances to a point of threatening a rise in price pressures and the Fed responds with three or more steps to restrain credit availability, you should sell your bonds and invest half the proceeds in 3-month Treasury bills and half in 5-year Treasury notes. Conversely, when a cyclical downturn threatens to evolve into a full-blown recession and the Fed counters with three or more steps to increase the supply of credit, you should sell your Treasury bills and 5-year notes and use the proceeds to buy long-term bonds.

Turning to the first two analytical tricks, let's look first at the direction and magnitude of changes in the "sacred seven" in a contemporary context. Let's say we've seen an upturn signaled by strong gains for several consecutive months in a majority of the "sacred seven" indicators, including factory durable goods orders, supplier deliveries, industrial production, and nonfarm payrolls. Specifically, factory durable goods orders and supplier deliveries tend to lead the pack by being the earliest to advance, then industrial production and nonfarm payrolls tend to follow with strong gains. (There is no hard and fast rule for identifying strong gains in orders and production, but several consecutive months of growth in excess of 0.5% might qualify.)

Another analytical trick is that of identifying consistent upward (or downward) revisions in the initial estimates of economic data which you are scrutinizing. Of course, a string of monthly upward revised increases in any of the "sacred seven" economic sign posts could signal that a recovery is underway. An excellent example was the revised March 1994 increase of 0.8% in durable goods orders, which represented a significant upward adjustment from the initial estimate of 0.4%. This represented the seventh increase in this series over eight months. (Most of the "sacred seven" indicators are revised in the subsequent month or two on the scheduled monthly release dates.) Look for particularly hefty revisions in the monthly nonfarm payroll employment series. Large revisions in the nonfarm payroll figures are virtually guaranteed by the fact that only about 50% of the 360,000 businesses surveyed each month for this series report initially. Following the initial estimate of monthly nonfarm payrolls there are two subsequent monthly revisions as the sample of reporting businesses becomes more complete. It should be noted, however, that the market response to the initial monthly nonfarm payroll estimate is usually the strongest one. A good illustration of upward revisions in nonfarm payroll figures pointing to a strengthening in economic activity came in April 1994. Originally, the increase in April nonfarm payrolls was estimated by the Bureau of Labor Statistics to be an already respectable 267,000. Subse-quently, this increase was revised to show a much larger 358,000 increase, and this figure was revised a second time to a huge 401,000 increase. As a rule, you will find that any string of consistent upward (or downward) revisions in estimates of nonfarm payroll employment is usually a reliable signal of economic ups and downs. (The only component of the "sacred seven" not typically revised is commodity prices.)

A fourth analytical trick is the more abstract attempt to spot self-reinforcing tendencies in key economic indicators. For example, several successive monthly increases in new orders will lead to sustained strength in production, which, in turn, eventually leads to increased employment and stronger income growth. In this self-reinforcing process, we have the makings of a vigorous and prolonged recovery. The self-sustaining feature of this process stems from the fact that the resulting higher-income growth will, in turn, lead to higher spending, which will lead to faster depletion of business inventories. Subsequently, as businesses seek to rebuild their inventories, they will increase new orders, supplier delivery lead times will lengthen, and industrial production will increase, thus giving a further boost to this self-reinforcing recovery process.

The final analytical trick consists of searching out evidence of demand-induced shortages in skilled labor or productive capacity limits as the recovery approaches its peak. Shortages of skilled labor or high rates of industrial capacity utilization can lead to increased wages and prices and, more important, to inflationary conditions that can rock your bond and stock holdings. The best place to look for early evidence of these trends is in the Federal Reserve's beige book, released two weeks before each of the eight regularly scheduled Federal Open Market Committee (FOMC) meetings each year. (The annual schedule for these FOMC meetings is available from the public information department of the Federal Reserve Board of Governors in Washington, D.C.) The beige book covers economic developments and regional anecdotal information in each of the 12 Fed districts. The first signs in the current recovery that some firms were operating near capacity came in the April 1994 beige book. It noted, in particular, that production of autos, vehicle parts, steel, and building materials was near capacity. Scattered shortages of skilled labor had previously been noted in the January 1994 beige book and again in subsequent surveys during the year.

WATCHING IMPORT LEVELS

You should remember that high growth doesn't necessarily translate immediately into accelerating price pressures. Early in any recovery, for example, when a large measure of industrial capacity is unused and the unemployment rate is relatively high, there is leeway for a spurt in growth without immediate inflationary consequences. Also, accelerating demand growth may be sustained without an immediate acceleration in price pressures when it spills over, as in the current recovery, into increased imports from major industrial trading partners that happen to have substantial margins of unused productive capacity and labor. Of course, you should be aware in this latter case that a mounting U.S. trade deficit would likely exert downward pressure on the dollar and upward pressure on import prices, thus at some point leading to escalating inflationary pressures.

Under normal circumstances, there are certain "comfort zones" of real GDP growth that you should keep in mind. Currently, based on projected trends in labor force and productivity growth, the United States could grow at a rate of 2.6% per year without seeing significant inflation. The monetary authorities use this benchmark for the economy's sustainable longer-term growth to guide their policy. As long as they are convinced that this level of economic growth will be sustained, Fed officials will tend to keep their policy stance unchanged. If, on the other hand, they see GDP growth slow to 1% or less they will take steps to boost the economy through expanding credit and decreasing interest rates in order to avert the onset of a recession. Alternatively, an acceleration in real GDP growth to 4% or higher threatens an acceleration in the inflation rate, especially when we're reaching the limits of production capacity. This could prompt the Fed to curtail credit and to raise its cost.

INVESTING IN A "BALANCE SHEET" RECOVERY

In addition to cyclical turning points, you need to watch for certain distinguishing features of recoveries (or recessions) that may have a bearing on Fed actions. In the late 1970s, for example, inflation psychology was seemingly intractable, necessitating aggressive Fed actions to curtail credit availability that pushed interest rates up to record highs and plunged stock and bond market fortunes to dismal lows. Workers worried that future excessive increases in prices of goods and services would continue to erode their purchasing power. This caused them to hike unit labor costs by demanding wage increases well in excess of the growth in their productivity (output per worker hour). Likewise, consumers eagerly speculated in commodities and real estate in anticipation of quick profits occasioned by anticipated near-term price increases. Similarly, businesses bid aggressively for raw materials and engaged in speculative inventory buildups and excessive spending on land and structures in anticipation of future price increases. To counter this behavior the Fed had to tighten credit availability and elevate short-term money market interest rates to a point that had a devastating impact on bond and stock holdings.

In contrast, in the early 1990s, the distinguishing feature was a "balance sheet" problem of major proportions. Both consumers and businesses suffered declines in their wealth as prices declined in real estate and other real assets inflated excessively in the 1980s. At the same time, consumers and businesses suffered from stifling debt burdens arising mainly from real estate speculation and other excesses such as the mergers and acquisitions mania of the 1980s.

Fed Chairman Alan Greenspan aptly characterized this recovery's unusual balance sheet problems as the economy's 50-mile-per-hour "head wind." Appropriately, Greenspan saw the need for the Fed to slowly expand the supply of credit in measured steps over a protracted period (the Fed executed 25 easing steps from June 1989 through September 1992) and then for the monetary authorities to maintain a friendly or "quite accommodative" policy stance unusually far into the current recovery (from September 1992 until early February 1994). Against this background of declining interest rates, individuals refinanced home mortgages and paid down their debts (four major waves of mortgage refinancings took place from late 1991 to mid-1993). Similarly, businesses were able to refinance their debt and even to repay some of this debt with funds raised in the rallying stock market. In this environment, consumer and business spending was curtailed and disinflationary psychology reined supreme.

The balance sheet aspects of this recovery gave all investors a once-in-a-lifetime opportunity to make big money on bonds and stocks. Its environment of moderate growth and declining inflation were ideal for both the bond and stock markets and they rallied together unusually far into the current recovery. What many did not realize, however, was that this was a prolonged period of abundant credit available at attractive terms for virtually all borrowers, including global speculators. Conditions were ripe for bond and stock market excesses from which you as an individual investor had to be ready to protect yourself. In 1993, for example, large institutional investors such as hedge funds, mutual funds, and pension funds made big global bets in debt, equity, and currency markets. As an individual investor in mutual funds, you had to worry that this intense speculation by big institutional players, many of whom were capable of making greatly leveraged bets, would extend both the U.S. and foreign bond and stock market rallies beyond levels justified by economic fundamentals. Although it may be customary to blame eager individual investors for market excesses, this time it appeared to be mainly the big, leveraged global speculators that extended the bond and stock market rallies to excessive and dangerous territory. When you sense that these excesses are emerging, you should take some profits in your bond and stock holdings and build up your cash holdings.

As an individual investor you must always be on guard for excesses in stock and bond market rallies. Most important, when financial market excesses arise, you must anticipate that the Fed may be on the verge of reversing its easy credit policies. Obviously, a sudden Fed shift to a more restrictive policy that curtails credit availability and pushes short-term interest rates higher will have an immediate negative impact on bond and stock market fortunes and thus on the value of your investment portfolio. Such Fed restrictive policy shifts should serve as the key to major portfolio shifts out of bonds into cash. A second reason to be aware of excesses in stock and bond market rallies is that the higher they go, the harder they will fall. You can save yourself a lot of sleepless nights if you act early in making prudent portfolio adjustments.

PERSONAL OBSERVATIONS TO HELP IDENTIFY CYCLICAL TURNING POINTS

In your effort to diagnose the health of the economy, you would be well advised to use your own personal observations, in addition to the "sacred seven" economic indicators, to help identify cyclical turning points. Real-life sources include, as noted earlier, taxi drivers, real estate agents, or retail sales clerks in your own hometown or on the road when you are traveling. (One taxi driver told me recently that while he didn't have an opinion on the business outlook, he did have an opinion on economists—they should all be shot.)

While your conversation with these people can reveal a lot about your local economy, it is important not to rely on this information alone. Let's say, for instance, you were trying to judge the vigor of Christmas spending as a measure of the economy's health. The idea is, of course, to use this additional information on the economy's vigor to determine when Fed policy is about to shift and, in turn, to make the appropriate adjustments in your investment portfolio.

If you looked around during the holiday season, you might see large crowds in department stores or the lack of space in shopping mall parking lots during the shopping days before Christmas. The problem is that crowd size tells you very little about average spending per person. During recession, people will spend less per person than during recoveries when confidence, jobs, and income are growing. The answer is to check these important personal observations against the results from the "sacred seven" indicators to get a full economic picture that helps you to anticipate Fed policy shifts.

2

Understanding Inflation Psychology

Now that you have a handle on the economy's turning points, you must take a look at one more general consideration crucial to your investment success. More than anything else, the longer-term fate of your stock and bond portfolio rides on inflation psychology or the collective judgment of your fellow large and small investors regarding future expected inflationary pressures over the coming decade or so. The harsh reality is that investors in bond obligations who receive a fixed periodic payment of interest income by bond issuers can be hurt badly by future increases in inflationary pressures, because higher inflation diminishes the buying power of the investor's fixed interest income. Therefore, if investors collectively believe that future inflationary pressures are going to increase over the longer run, these expectations will tend to be reflected in a rising inflation premium that is extracted from borrowers in the bond market in the form of a higher bond yield. Rising bond yields, in turn, make alternative investments in stocks less attractive. This happened, for example, in the 1970s when there was the belief among investors (and others) that rising inflation would continue for a considerable period into the future. These inflation expectations were reflected in climbing interest rates on debt obligations (see Figure 2.1), and the stock market faltered accordingly.

In contrast, when investors believe that price pressures will decline for some considerable time into the future, these expectations will be reflected in declining bond yields and rising stock prices, as can be seen in the 1980s and early 1990s. In particular, it should be

Figure 2.1   **10-Year Note Yield and Consumer Price Index, 1960–1994**

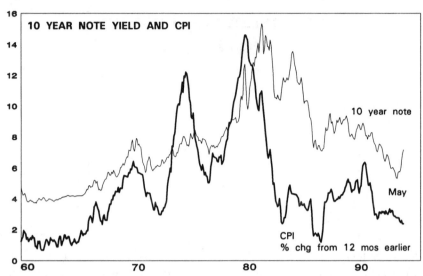

Source: Federal Reserve and U.S. Bureau of Labor Statistics.

noted that declining investor inflation expectations were a crucial ingredient in the 1993 bond and stock market rallies.

To be sure, there is in the short-run a trade-off between growth in real economic output and prices. For example, a combination of tight credit and high interest rates will curtail consumer demand, which, in turn, depresses output and employment growth, resulting in lower inflation. Nevertheless, in the longer run (i.e., periods of 10 years or longer), the government cannot necessarily buy lower inflation with higher unemployment. In fact, in the longer run, there must be a combination of a strong, anti-inflation governmental policy and confidence in continued stable prices to keep bond investor inflation expectations in check. Low inflation expectations will, in turn, be reflected in low long-term interest rates, which will set the stage for sustainable longer-term growth in economic activity.

This chapter will show you what conditions are like when inflationary pressures are getting out of control, as in the 1970s. Not only did the Fed fail to adequately restrain credit during most of this decade, but there were also oil price shocks in 1973 and again in 1979. During such periods when inflation expectations are escalating, your holdings of bonds and stocks will face rough sledding, and you may spend more than a few sleepless nights unless you make the appropriate portfolio adjustments. In contrast, when inflation expectations are diminishing, as happened through most of the 1980s and the early 1990s, investors who bet heavily on financial assets like bonds and stocks will sleep soundly with visions of capital gains and personal financial independence dancing in their heads.

THE GOVERNMENT'S INFLATION-FIGHTING CREDIBILITY AND INFLATIONARY SENTIMENT

The government has a difficult time winning the public's confidence that it can control inflation. If it loses that credibility, it is extremely hard to regain. The loss of government's anti-inflation credibility creates a fertile environment for the escalation of investor fears of higher inflation. Investors as a group know that once the government lets inflationary pressures get out of control, they must adjust their investment portfolios accordingly. If inflation expectations are increasing, you should lighten up on financial assets like stocks and bonds in favor of real assets like real estate and natural resources. Rising inflation expectations will be reflected in higher bond yields as new fixed-income investors seek to protect the purchasing power of their fixed interest income. Moreover, as rising nominal yields on bond investments become more attractive, alternative investment in stocks will become less attractive. In addition, rising interest rates during periods of tight credit will eventually curtail economic activity and depress earnings growth, thus multiplying stock market woes.

It's mainly the Fed's job to protect the credibility of the government's stance against inflation. And yet, when the federal government adheres to a strict budget, it makes the Fed's task a lot easier. This was evident in the late 1950s when budget surpluses (praise the thought) complemented recurring periods of monetary restraint (see Chapter 3). During this period, recurring doses of Fed tightening in the supply of credit, combined with balanced-budget fiscal discipline, helped set the stage for a golden period of economic growth with low inflation and subdued inflation expectations in the early 1960s. These conditions prevailed because the public believed in the government's ability to keep inflation in check. As a result, investors kept their inflation expectations in check, and long-term interest rates remained sufficiently low to sustain solid economic growth.

In contrast, the government began to lose its anti-inflation credibility in the second half of the 1960s. This loss of credibility began on the fiscal side when the Johnson administration deliberately understated the extent of the buildup in defense spending associated with escalating the Vietnam war. The Johnson administration was at that time emphasizing a fiscally irresponsible "guns and butter" spending approach whereby it increased both defense spending in support of the Vietnam war and Great Society spending programs in support of a domestic war on poverty.

To make matters worse, government anti-inflation credibility was further damaged when Fed Chairman Martin, after a long and distinguished performance as Fed chairman, made an error in judgment. He prematurely eased monetary policy in response to a belated Johnson administration tax increase in 1968. The Martin Fed acted on the mistaken assumption that the 1968 tax increase (required to help finance the Vietnam war) would promptly depress U.S. economic activity. Instead, the economy kept advancing, and the Fed's ill-timed easing step fanned inflationary pressures. As government anti-inflation credibility crumbled and investor inflation expectations increased in the second half of the 1960s, long-term interest rates began to rise.

THE IMPACT OF RUNAWAY INFLATION PSYCHOLOGY

A loss of confidence in the government's anti-inflation vigilance will result in runaway inflationary psychology with a self-sustaining momentum that is extremely difficult to break. For example, as inflationary expectations soared in the 1970s, consumers began to speculate in real assets, anticipating future price increases. This was particularly the case in real estate when people bought two or more homes both as residences and investments. Land speculation was also rampant. Consumers took on excessive debt burdens in support of this speculative spending binge, on the correct assumption that rising inflation benefits debtors, who can sell their assets at inflated prices, and penalizes lenders, who are paid back in inflation-cheapened dollars. Likewise, businesses borrowed heavily to support stepped-up spending on such real assets as inventories, land,

and office and plant structures which were expected to appreciate dramatically in value in line with sharply rising price pressures.

In this environment of runaway inflation psychology, workers demanded large wage increases far in excess of their productivity in order to try to stay ahead of expected increases in their cost of living. Unit labor costs mushroomed, reinforcing increased price pressures.

At this point, investors will begin to expect that inflationary pressures will continue to increase and they will build an inflation premium into bond yields necessary to induce them to buy new debt obligations. Once fixed-income investors have been badly burned by out-of-control price pressures, and they build this inflationary premium into nominal bond yields, it tends to stubbornly persist. Only if investors become absolutely certain that government anti-inflation credibility is restored and that price pressures are moderating will this inflation premium be reduced. The bottom line is that when you and your fellow individual investors believe that future inflationary pressures will increase over a prolonged period, you should scale down your holdings of financial assets like stocks and bonds.

IDENTIFYING FEATURES OF ESCALATING INFLATIONARY PSYCHOLOGY

As an investor in financial assets like stocks and bonds who is threatened with significant portfolio losses in periods of escalating inflation expectations, you need to watch for certain important sign posts of sustained and pervasive price pressures. The first sign of strengthening consumer demand for goods and services in a recovery can be found in rising prices of commodities and raw materials used in the production process. But you should remember that commodity prices are notoriously volatile—affected by a host of outside factors like weather, earthquakes, and wars—and account for less than one-third of the cost of production. More than two-thirds of the cost of production is accounted for by labor costs. Wage demands will increase when the unemployment rate falls below the "natural" level and pockets of skilled labor shortages begin to multiply. In these circumstances wage demands and strike activity will usually accelerate sharply. (The "natural" unemployment level, currently about 5$^1/_2$%, is the lowest level to which the employment rate can be pushed without triggering rising wage and price pressures.) The "natural" unemployment rate is fairly high because of a mismatch between a large pool of unskilled workers and jobs requiring increasing skills and education.

One hint that wage demands are accelerating can be found in accelerating monthly increases in average hourly earnings (see Figure 2.2). This report is released on the first Friday of each month along with the nonfarm payroll and household employment reports by the Bureau of Labor Statistics. An accelerating trend in average hourly earnings occurred during the period from 1965 through the early 1980s. Eventually, when the rate of increase in wages and benefits exceeds the rate of increase of productivity (output per worker hour), then unit labor costs will rise, exerting upward pressure on producer and consumer prices. A good way for you to confirm a trend in rising price pressures that could lead to escalating inflation psychology is to watch for an acceleration in annual rates of increase in consumer prices over several years (see Table 2.1). Note that in 1968–70 there was a clear indication of an acceleration in consumer prices that was destined to persist throughout the 1970s. In contrast, during 1982–84 there was a de-

Figure 2.2   Average Hourly Earnings, 1965–1993 (Percentage Change from 12 Months Earlier)

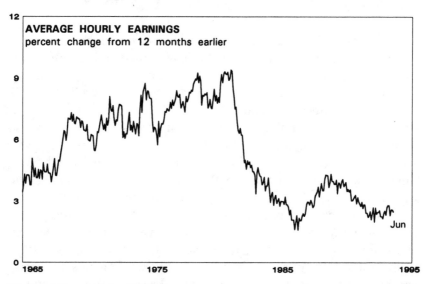

Source: U.S. Bureau of Labor Statistics.

Table 2.1 **Consumer Prices, 1960–1993**

Year	Percentage Change over 12 Months	Year	Percentage Change over 12 Months
1960	1.4	1980	12.4
1961	0.7	1981	8.9
1962	1.2	1982	3.8
1963	1.6	1983	3.8
1964	1.2	1984	4.0
1965	1.9	1985	3.8
1966	3.4	1986	1.2
1967	3.3	1987	4.4
1968	4.7	1988	4.4
1969	5.9	1989	4.6
1970	5.6	1990	6.3
1971	3.3	1991	3.0
1972	3.4	1992	3.0
1973	8.9	1993	2.7
1974	12.1		
1975	7.1		
1976	5.0		
1977	6.7		
1978	9.0		
1979	13.3		

Source: U.S. Bureau of Labor Statistics.

celeration in the rate of increase in consumer prices that signaled a declining trend which persisted through the 1980s into the early 1990s. The continuing downward drift in inflation expectations in the early 1990s is evident in Figure 2.3 which is based on a survey of expected inflation over the subsequent 10 years, published by the Federal Reserve Bank of Philadelphia.

DISINFLATIONARY PSYCHOLOGY HELPS FUEL MARKET RALLIES

Bold anti-inflation strokes by the government that serve to break the back of inflation psychology will help set the stage for longer-term bond and stock market rallies. Sometimes the government uses both symbolism and substantive anti-inflationary measures that are truly effective. Two examples are President Ronald Reagan's bold and symbolic action in 1981 to fire the striking

Figure 2.3   **Inflation Expectations, 1991–1994**

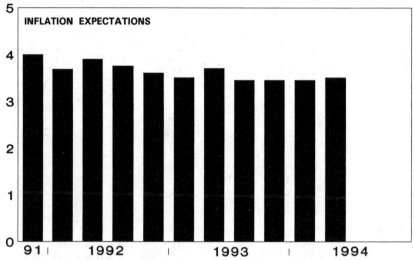

Economists' quarterly forecasts of the average annual increase in
consumer prices over the subsequent 10 years.

Source: Federal Reserve Bank of Philadelphia.

flight controllers, a highly publicized act that set the stage for a
weakening in union power and a deescalation in wage demands in
the 1980s.

Also helping to convincingly rehabilitate government anti-
inflation credibility in the early 1980s was Fed Chairman Paul
Volcker's heroic and successful battle against inflation. Volcker's
clamp-down on credit availability produced a surge in interest rates
to record levels (the prime rate hit a peak of 21.5% in late 1980).
These tight credit conditions brought about a weakening in consumer and business spending and rising unemployment. Volcker's
extreme credit restraint was so powerful that it helped produce two
back-to-back recessions, a brief one lasting from February 1980 to
July 1980 and a long and deep one lasting from August 1981 to
November 1982. The rate of increase in producer and consumer
prices generally declined over the course of the 1980s and was reinforced by the oil price collapse in 1986.

In any case, the decisive anti-inflation actions by Reagan and
Volcker helped set the stage for declining price pressures (see Figure
2.4) and falling inflation expectations in the 1980s and early

Figure 2.4 **Inflation Measures, 1960–1994 (Percentage Change from 4 Quarters Earlier)**

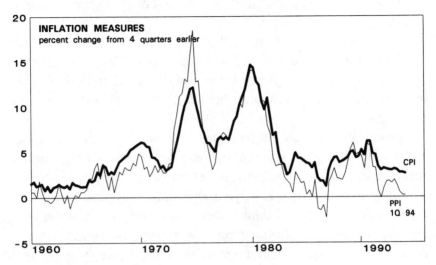

Source: U.S. Bureau of Labor Statistics.

1990s. Deregulation in the transportation industry and foreign competition, especially in the auto industry, helped curtail wage and price pressures. In turn, these declining wage and price pressures eventually caused investors to believe that future inflationary pressures were on the wane. This decline in investor inflation psychology was associated with a downward trend in long-term interest rates in the 1980s and early 1990s, providing fertile conditions for a prosperous decade for stock and bond investors. These blissful conditions for investors climaxed with the spectacular bond and stock market rallies in 1993.

INVESTING IN AN ENVIRONMENT OF DISINFLATIONARY PSYCHOLOGY

When trying to get a handle on inflation psychology you should think of major trends in wage and price pressures during periods of 10 years or longer. Inflationary psychology is thus the broad backdrop for your personal investment decisions. It might be thought of as the canvas on which you will paint your particular investment landscape. For example, in an environment of disinflationary psychology, you and your fellow individual investors should tilt your portfolio in favor of financial assets including both bonds and stocks.

To determine if you are still in a disinflationary environment, you should watch the annual percentage change in average hourly earnings and consumer prices. If the rate of growth in both average hourly earnings and consumer prices declines during a string of several years in a row, you are in all likelihood in a disinflationary environment and you should load up on financial assets like stocks and bonds. But when the rate of increase in both average hourly earnings and consumer prices reverses course and begins to accelerate for several years in a row, your environment is probably changing. You should begin to think about selling your bonds and investing the proceeds in shorter-term investments and redeploying a portion of your equity holdings into natural resource stocks or real estate which will appreciate in conditions of rising price pressures and escalating longer-term inflation expectations.

A useful rule of thumb when you decide that conditions are right for stocks and bonds is that you should adjust the proportion of stocks and bonds in your portfolio primarily according to your main investment risk-return preference and time horizon. Accordingly, if you are not afraid of risk and have a long investment horizon, your proportion of stocks might be high and bonds low. The idea is to build your savings nest egg through a strong-appreciation portfolio strategy by taking more risk but with the chance of higher returns. Alternatively, if you have a stomach for only moderate risk and an intermediate-term investment horizon (perhaps as do the bulk of readers of this book), and have accumulated a hefty savings nest egg already, you should strike a more balanced risk-return approach by establishing approximately an equal balance between stocks and bonds. Finally, if you have little stomach for risk and a relatively short-term investment horizon, you should follow an income-oriented investment strategy in which the bulk of your portfolio might be invested in bonds and only a modest portion in stocks.

Section Two

WHAT YOU NEED TO KNOW
ABOUT WASHINGTON'S POLICIES
AND POLITICS

A s an investor, there is no way you can ignore Washington's personalities and politics. But there are some things that you should watch more closely than others; namely the government's fiscal discipline and Fed policy initiatives. Regarding government taxes and spending, you need to focus on whether the public believes that the current administration is handling finances in a responsible manner. Specifically, you want to know whether the country can maintain the interest payments on our large public debt total and seemingly endless annual deficits (expenditures in excess of tax receipts) that add continuously to this debt total. If it appears federal debt servicing requirements will outstrip the rate of growth in the nation's tax base (GDP), then you could face capital losses on your bond holdings. You can spot that trend in its developmental phases. Look for a persistently rising ratio of the deficit to GDP.

Even as you keep a watch on the government's spending habits, you must keep an eye trained on the Federal Reserve. Above all, your investment fortunes are tied to the secretive deliberations and actions of the monetary authorities. This section will help you peel away the layers of misunderstanding shrouding the Fed, so that you can use Fed policy actions to your advantage in managing your investments. Our motto as Fed watchers is to watch what the Fed actually watches, not what you think it should watch.

In the past, the Fed has used the money supply as the most reliable indicator of impending inflation problems. More recently, however, Fed officials have come to rely less on money and more on such early inflation signals as general commodity price increases, lengthening delivery lead times along with efforts to increase inventories, and accelerating credit growth.

The Fed's primary objective is stable prices, because stable prices are a prerequisite to sustainable long-term economic growth. The policymakers are continuously diagnosing the economy on the basis of incoming financial and economic data. In formulating monetary policy, Fed authorities respond partly to current developments and partly to anticipated future trends.

Starting on February 4, 1994, the Fed has begun a series of moderate steps to tighten up on the supply of credit (the funds you can borrow from banks or nonbank sources to buy cars, homes, or for other purposes). These Fed-tightening steps came against the backdrop of strengthening economic recovery and a potential acceleration in long-dormant inflationary pressures.

When the Fed eases, or increases, the supply of credit in response to signs of a weakening economy and dormant price pressures, short-term interest rates will decline immediately and long-term interest rates, depending on the degree of fiscal discipline, the behavior of the dollar, and inflation expectations, will usually decline afterward. But long-term interest rates will customarily decline by a smaller amount than short-term interest rates. Declining interest rates make stocks increasingly attractive as an alternative investment. Declining interest rates also stimulate economic activity and, in turn, boost corporate earnings, which in turn enhances stock values. Cash, or other short-term liquid investments, are least desirable to hold when the Fed is engaging in a series of easing steps. This is because short-term interest rates payable on these liquid investments decline in lock-step with Fed-easing moves. Instead, you should invest your entire portfolio in stocks and long-term bonds, balanced according to your investment objective and time horizon.

Alternatively, if the Fed is engaging in a series of steps to tighten the supply of credit in response to a strengthening recovery and the threat of rising price pressures, short-term interest rates will increase immediately and long-term interest rates, again depending on the degree of fiscal discipline, the behavior of the dollar, and inflationary expectations, will typically follow later on. In this case, cash or short-term investments are desirable because short-term interest rates will move up in lock-step with Fed-tightening moves. Thus, you might consider redeeming all your long-term bonds and placing half the proceeds in shorter term 2- to 5-year fixed-income obligations (in order to earn a still fairly respectable interest rate) and half in lower rate but more liquid 3- to 6-month Treasury bills. Regarding your equity holdings, don't panic when the Fed starts tightening, but do be prepared for near-term losses. Remember, the investment idea offered in this book is to maximize your investment returns in favorable market circumstances and to minimize your losses in unfavorable conditions.

Just the same, there are times when you might consider shifting part of your equity portfolio into real assets. For example, if the Fed, perhaps because of undue political pressures, doesn't move quickly enough to keep inflation in check, you should consider shifting perhaps as much as 25% of your equity holdings into real assets such as real estate or natural resources. An alternative is to shift holdings into oil or gold sector mutual funds or preferably general natural resource mutual funds that would benefit from escalating inflationary expectations.

Since the Fed chairman's job is highly political, it is extremely important to understand the nature of the relationship between the Fed chairman and the White House. The relationship is important because the Fed needs to be free from undue political pressure to effectively carry out its primary policy aim of stable prices. If the Fed and the White House are at odds, inflationary pressures may get out of control and your stock and bond investments will hit the skids.

When the Fed takes the politically undesirable action of tightening credit availability and raising interest rates, thus causing the administration's constituents to pay more for loans, the Fed is usually the object of a barrage of criticism from the Congress and the White House. If this political pressure is excessive, it could lead to delayed or inadequate Fed anti-inflation actions. Fortunately, the relationship between the Greenspan Fed and the Clinton administration has been remarkably amicable. This has given Chairman Greenspan adequate leeway in 1994 to begin to try to tighten credit sufficiently to keep inflation in check.

Somewhat surprisingly, Fed Chairman Alan Greenspan, the serious, urbane, cultured, introverted, Republican New Yorker, has hit it off well personally with the extroverted, Elvis Presley–loving, Southern Democratic politician who now occupies the White House. Perhaps this is because both men are "intellectual pragmatists" who love detail and savor endless discussions of historical perspective and policy options. The positive relationship between Clinton and the Fed has given the Fed leeway to make a preemptive strike against inflation in 1994.

Although the Fed's relationship with Congress is also important—the Fed is actually an independent agency of the legislative branch—the critical relationship between the Fed and the White House usually determines whether the monetary authorities will have the leeway to restrain credit availability sufficiently to keep inflation in check. To be sure, the Fed is independent within the government's policy framework and is thus able to act at its own discretion to engage in actions to tighten (or ease) the supply of credit. Nevertheless, undue political pressure on the Fed can cause the monetary authorities to delay or be too timid in tightening actions required to keep inflationary pressures in check.

3

How the Budget Battles Influence Your Bond Investments

The old budget-deficit bugaboo can hound you as both a taxpayer and an investor. As an investor, realize that when economic recovery gets under way and government tax revenues are climbing, rising business and consumer credit demands may compete with the government's still fairly steep borrowing needs, thereby exerting upward pressure on interest rates. At the same time, however, you should also remember that rising federal deficits may not always result in climbing long-term interest rates; declining inflationary expectations can dampen that trend, as we saw in the 1980s, and decrease bond yields. Also, when the economy tilts over into recession and business and consumer credit demands are drying up, a rising deficit may be associated with declining bond yields, as in the 1990–91 recession.

GENERAL LINKAGES

The Fed influences short-term interest rates directly through its credit-easing or tightening actions (see Exhibit 3.1). However, the Fed alone has an indirect influence on long-term interest rates. Other forces influencing long-term interest rates include fiscal policy (taxes and spending), the dollar, and inflation expectations. Actually, fiscal policy affects long-term interest rates primarily through government demands on the capital markets to finance deficits (dissaving) and, most important, by longer-term investor

Exhibit 3.1 **Linkages Between Federal Reserve Policy, Inflation Expectations, Bond Yields, and Stock Prices**

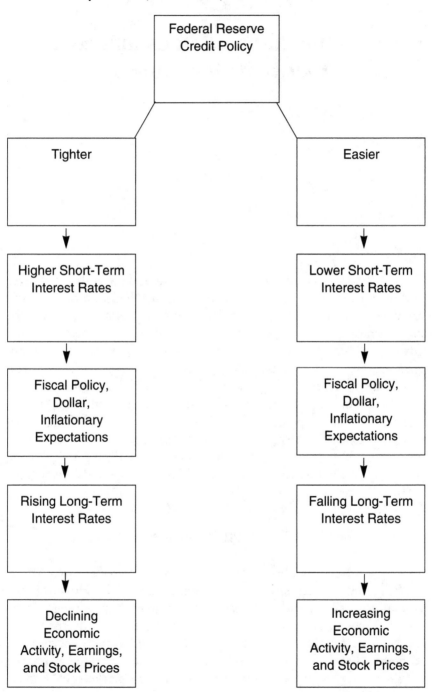

Federal Reserve Credit Policy

Tighter	Easier
Higher Short-Term Interest Rates	Lower Short-Term Interest Rates
Fiscal Policy, Dollar, Inflationary Expectations	Fiscal Policy, Dollar, Inflationary Expectations
Rising Long-Term Interest Rates	Falling Long-Term Interest Rates
Declining Economic Activity, Earnings, and Stock Prices	Increasing Economic Activity, Earnings, and Stock Prices

Source: Aubrey G. Lanston & Co., Inc.

fears that rising deficits may not be covered by growth in the tax base. When increasing private investment demands compete with rising government demands for a limited amount of domestic savings, upward pressure will be exerted on real long-term interest rates (nominal long-term interest rates less inflation expectations). Other conditions that may exert upward pressure on long-term interest rates are a declining trend in the dollar and rising inflation expectations.

When the Fed tightens the availability of credit, short-term interest rates will rise immediately and usually more sharply than the increase in long-term interest rates. Conversely, when the Fed is easing the supply of credit, short-term interest rates will decline immediately and usually more sharply than the decline in long-term interest rates.

Note in both Table 3.1 and Figure 3.1 that during recession periods like 1990–91 and 1981–82, federal debt expands sharply, reflecting slumping tax receipts and accelerating government antirecession spending programs like unemployment compensation. In 1990 and 1991, the deficit was also inflated by spending to pay off depositors at failed savings and loan associations. In contrast, con-

Figure 3.1 **Federal Government Budget Deficit, Fiscal 1970–1999**

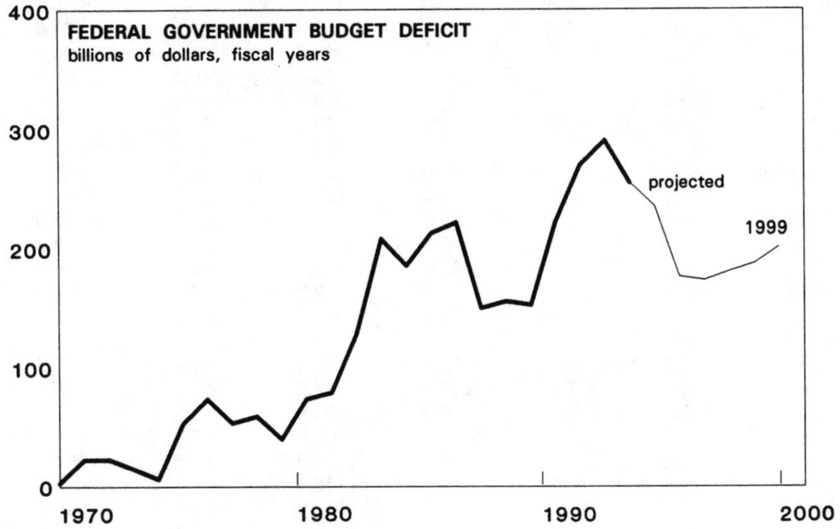

Source: U.S. Office of Management and Budget.

Table 3.1　**Federal Receipts, Outlays, Surplus or Deficit, and Debt,
Fiscal 1940–1995**

(Billions of Dollars)

Fiscal Year	Total			Gross Federal Debt (end of period)		Addendum: Gross Domestic Product
	Receipts	Outlays	Surplus or Deficit (–)	Total	Held by the Public	
1940	6.5	9.5	–2.9	50.7	42.8	95.4
1941	8.7	13.7	–4.9	57.5	48.2	112.5
1942	14.6	35.1	–20.5	79.2	67.8	141.8
1943	24.0	78.6	–54.6	142.6	127.8	175.4
1944	43.7	91.3	–47.6	204.1	184.8	201.7
1945	45.2	92.7	–47.6	260.1	235.2	212.0
1946	39.3	55.2	–15.9	271.0	241.9	212.5
1947	38.5	34.5	4.0	257.1	224.3	222.9
1948	41.6	29.8	11.8	252.0	216.3	246.7
1949	39.4	38.8	0.6	252.6	214.3	262.7
1950	39.4	42.6	–3.1	256.9	219.0	265.8
1951	51.6	45.5	6.1	255.3	214.3	313.5
1952	66.2	67.7	–1.5	259.1	214.8	340.5
1953	69.6	76.1	–6.5	266.0	218.4	363.8
1954	69.7	70.9	–1.2	270.8	224.5	368.0
1955	65.5	68.4	–3.0	274.4	226.6	384.7
1956	74.6	70.6	3.9	272.7	222.2	416.3
1957	80.0	76.6	3.4	272.3	219.3	483.3
1958	79.6	82.4	–2.8	279.7	226.3	448.1
1959	79.2	92.1	–12.8	287.5	234.7	480.2
1960	92.5	92.2	0.3	290.5	236.8	504.6
1961	94.4	97.7	–3.3	292.6	238.4	517.0
1962	99.7	106.8	–7.1	302.9	248.0	555.2
1963	106.6	111.3	–4.8	310.3	254.0	584.5
1964	112.6	118.5	–5.9	316.1	256.8	625.3
1965	116.8	118.2	–1.4	322.3	260.8	671.0
1966	130.8	134.5	–3.7	328.5	263.7	735.4
1967	148.8	157.5	–8.6	340.4	266.6	793.3
1968	153.0	178.1	–25.2	368.7	289.5	847.2
1969	186.9	183.6	3.2	365.8	278.1	925.7
1970	192.8	195.6	–2.8	380.9	283.2	985.4
1971	187.1	210.2	–23.0	408.2	303.0	1050.9
1972	207.3	230.7	–23.4	435.9	322.4	1147.8
1973	230.8	245.7	–14.9	466.3	340.9	1274.0
1974	263.2	269.4	–6.1	483.9	343.7	1403.6
1975	279.1	332.3	–53.2	541.9	394.7	1509.8
1976	298.1	371.8	–73.7	629.0	477.4	1684.2
Transition quarter	81.2	96.0	–14.7	643.6	495.5	445.0
1977	355.6	409.2	–53.7	706.4	549.1	1917.2
1978	399.6	458.7	–59.2	776.6	607.1	2155.0
1979	463.3	503.5	–40.2	828.9	639.8	2429.5
1980	517.1	590.9	–73.8	908.5	709.3	2644.1
1981	599.3	678.2	–79.0	994.3	784.8	2964.4
1982	617.8	745.8	–128.0	1136.8	919.2	3122.2
1983	600.6	808.4	–207.8	1371.2	1131.0	3316.5

(continued)

Table 3.1 **(Continued)**

(Billions of Dollars)

Fiscal Year	Total			Gross Federal Debt (end of period)		Addendum: Gross Domestic Product
	Receipts	Outlays	Surplus or Deficit (–)	Total	Held by the Public	
1984	666.5	851.8	–185.4	1564.1	1300.0	3695.0
1985	734.1	964.4	–212.3	1817.0	1499.4	3967.7
1986	769.1	990.3	–221.2	2120.1	1736.2	4219.0
1987	854.1	1003.9	–149.8	2345.6	1888.1	4452.4
1988	909.0	1064.1	–155.2	2600.8	2050.3	4808.4
1989	990.7	1143.2	–152.5	2867.5	2189.3	5173.3
1990	1031.3	1252.7	–221.4	3206.2	2410.4	5481.5
1991	1054.3	1323.8	–269.5	3598.3	2687.9	5673.3
1992	1090.5	1380.9	–290.4	4001.9	2998.6	5937.2
1993	1153.5	1408.2	–254.7	4351.2	3247.2	6294.8
1994[1]	1249.1	1483.8	–234.8	4676.0	3472.4	6641.2
1995[1]	1342.2	1518.3	–176.1	4960.1	3646.1	7022.0

[1]Estimates.
Source: U.S. Office of Management and Budget.

sumer and business debt expansion shows a pronounced slowing as spending weakens during such recession periods. Thus, despite rising government borrowing demands, recessions will typically produce a *lessening* in competition between government and private borrowing demands for a limited amount of domestic savings. That will usually lead to declining real long-term interest rates during recessions. Also exerting downward pressure on nominal long-term interest rates are declining inflation expectations. The latest bout of declining inflation expectations began in the 1980s and continued into the early 1990s.

LOWERING THE DEFICIT AND THE BOND MARKET REACTION

The Clinton administration has provided us with concrete evidence of the link between the deficit and the fate of our investments. From the very first days of its term, the Clinton administration made surprisingly aggressive efforts to cut the deficit and ultimately influenced the great bond market rally of 1993.

There were perhaps four turning points in Clinton's efforts to convince skeptics that he was serious about cutting the deficit.

Initially, it was expected that he would emphasize spending programs in typical Democratic party fashion. But at his postelection press conferences in Little Rock, Arkansas, the president-elect, on the advice of his senior economic advisors who championed the reaction of the bond market above all else, instead emphasized the need to cut the deficit. Given the disturbing history of rising deficits, for the Clinton administration to have a "credible" program in the eyes of bond market participants, its deficit-cutting efforts had to convincingly contribute to a projected decline in the ratio of the deficit to GDP in coming years. On the grand scale of historical political events, having a young, energetic Democratic president emphasize deficit-cutting, presumably with a multitude of new spending ideas in mind, was the equivalent of the anticommunist Republican President Richard Nixon's opening the door to communist China.

The Clinton administration's unexpected emphasis on future deficit-cutting actions in its early days had a major impact in getting the remarkable 1993 bond market rally started. As can be seen in Figure 3.2, long-term 30-year Treasury bond yields had backed up to 7.65% on November 3, 1992 (election day), because of investors' fears that the young Democratic challenger would break the budget with new spending programs. But bond investors were pleasantly surprised in the days immediately following the election as the president-elect repeatedly emphasized the need for aggressive deficit-cutting measures. The Clinton administration's predominant deficit-cutting theme helped push the long-term 30-year Treasury bond yield down to 6.90% by the end of February 1993.

The second high point in the Clinton administration's effort to convince investors that it would lower the deficit came soon after the presidential inauguration when Treasury Secretary Lloyd Bentsen appeared on NBC's "Meet the Press" television show in early 1993. Before millions of viewers, the Treasury Secretary mentioned that a broad-based energy tax "is on the table as an option to be considered." Given that President Clinton had rejected the energy tax during his campaign, from the bond market's viewpoint, this pronouncement lent more credibility to the Clinton administration's effort to cut the deficit and showed the influence that Treasury Secretary Bentsen's conservative, almost "Republican" economic team, carried in the new administration.

The third, significant deficit-cutting step came on February 17,

Figure 3.2 **Thirty-Year Bond Yields (Weekly), 1990–1994**

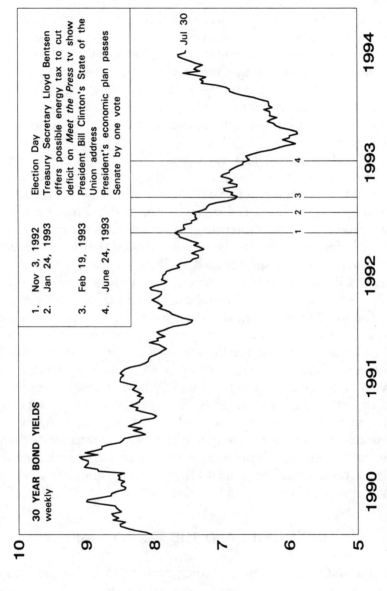

30 YEAR BOND YIELDS
weekly

1.	Nov 3, 1992	Election Day
2.	Jan 24, 1993	Treasury Secretary Lloyd Bentsen offers possible energy tax to cut deficit on *Meet the Press* tv show
3.	Feb 19, 1993	President Bill Clinton's State of the Union address
4.	June 24, 1993	President's economic plan passes Senate by one vote

Jul 30

Source: Federal Reserve and Aubrey G. Lanston & Co., Inc.

1993, with President Clinton's well-received State of the Union message detailing his economic plan. With Fed Chairman Greenspan in attendance (sitting between the president's and vice president's wives), the president took this opportunity to emphasize again the need for deficit reduction, while at the same time offering a moderate economic stimulus plan. Around this time, Clinton's commitment to increasing revenues through a seemingly endless series of contemplated tax increases (such as the energy tax and sin taxes) leaked through *The Wall Street Journal* and other newspapers, lent even more strength to the impression that he would cut the deficit.

The fourth highlight came with Federal Reserve Chairman Greenspan's favorable comments on the president's deficit-cutting plan. In his Humphrey-Hawkins congressional testimony on February 19, 1993, the Fed chairman stated that President Clinton was to be commended for placing a serious deficit-cutting plan on the table for active debate. Greenspan stressed that we must reduce the structural deficit sharply, and he observed that the Clinton plan was based on plausible economic assumptions and was appropriately specific in actions to be taken. The Fed chairman's praise for the Clinton deficit-cutting effort seemed to lend an increased air of credibility to the new administration's economic plan in general.

Clinton could see for himself how important it was that his economic program be perceived as being credible by bond market investors. Specifically, Clinton found that every time he emphasized deficit cutting in his early press contacts, the bond market would rally, and that the improving bond market was, in turn, having a favorable impact on the equity market. The idea was that by maintaining "credibility" in the bond market, stubbornly high long-term interest rates would be pushed lower, thereby stimulating business investment and housing and boosting economic growth.

THE BUDGET AND THE EQUITY MARKET

For the individual investor holding both bond and equity mutual funds in the early days of the Clinton administration, it was important to know something about not only the direct impact of the new president's deficit-cutting efforts on bond yields but also how the stock market might behave. There are special conditions in which both the bond and stock markets can rally together on a sustained basis. Foremost among these conditions are a persistent decline in investor inflation expectations (see Chapter 2), easy credit conditions, and sustained economic recovery with good earnings prospects through cost control. In 1993, these conditions merged perfectly to produce the spectacular bond and stock market rallies. Moreover, in order to produce the easy credit conditions, the Fed had pushed short-term interest rates down to levels that had caused a host of individual investors to shift out of low-yielding bank CDs into bond and stock mutual funds, thus reinforcing the bond and stock market rallies.

The impact of the Clinton administration's unexpectedly aggressive budget deficit-cutting measures on the equity market took place mostly indirectly through the positive impact of these actions on the bond market. Specifically, the deficit-cutting efforts triggered declines in bond yields, which, in turn, made investment in alternative stock holdings more attractive. In addition, declining long-term interest rates stimulated economic activity and improved earnings prospects.

Of course, the stock and bond markets have not always moved in such magnificent conformity. For example, there was a glaring exception in October 1987 when the stock market crashed and the bond market rallied on fears that the economy might tumble into a deep recession, or even depression, as in the October 1929 crash. In this case, the counterforce to the 1987 plunge in stock prices was a huge bond market rally, pushing 30-year Treasury bond yields down to $8^{1}/_{2}\%$ from roughly 10% within a matter of days.

THE HISTORY OF OUT-OF-CONTROL DEFICITS

From your point of view as an investor, there is only one critical budget issue: Will future deficits mushroom beyond the economy's capacity to service the debt through increased revenues? Specifically, the real danger occurs when, against the background of an already huge total amount of public debt outstanding, fiscal irresponsibility continues to prevail as the rate of growth of federal expenditures routinely exceeds the rate of growth of the tax base

(GDP). Ultimately, this undersirable fiscal condition will be reflected in a persistently rising ratio of the deficit to GDP.

To be sure, the U.S. picture has not been a pretty one. We had only had 5 years of budget surplus (tax revenues in excess of expenditures) in the 43 years since 1950. Nevertheless, there is hope in the belated resolve of Congress and the White House to curb the deficit, pushing the ratio of the deficit to GDP down from a four and a half decade high of 6.3% of GDP in 1983 to a projected 2.5% by 1995 (see both Figure 3.3 and Table 3.2).

In the past, the main budget problem in Washington, D.C., has been that Congress does not like to say "no" to its constituents, and consequently, we live beyond our means. Good examples of giveaway programs that started with good intentions and then spiraled out of control are the Medicare and Medicaid health programs (see Figure 3.4). However, when combined with a large Reagan tax cut and Congress's inability (or unwillingness) to cut nondefense spending sufficiently to make room for a massive defense buildup, deficits soared, boosting total public debt outstanding to more than $4 trillion in 1993 from just under $1 trillion in 1980. (Of this total, approximately $3 billion in debt outstanding

Figure 3.3   **Deficit as a Percentage of GDP, 1970–1999**

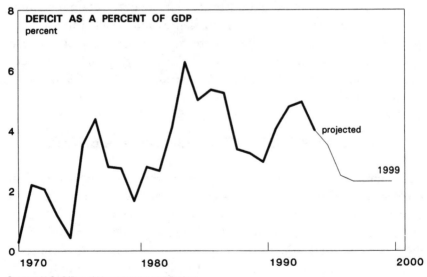

Source: U.S. Office of Management and Budget.

Table 3.2 **Federal Budget Receipts, Outlays, Surplus or Deficit, and Debt as Percentages of Gross Domestic Product, Fiscal Years 1940–1995**

Fiscal Year	Receipts	Outlays		Surplus or Deficit (−)	Gross Federal Debt (end of period)	
		Total	National Defense		Total	Held by Public
1940	6.9	9.9	1.7	−3.1	53.1	44.8
1941	7.7	12.1	5.7	−4.4	51.1	42.9
1942	10.3	24.8	18.1	−14.5	55.9	47.8
1943	13.7	44.8	38.0	−31.1	81.3	72.8
1944	21.7	45.3	39.2	−23.6	101.2	91.6
1945	21.3	43.7	39.1	−22.4	122.7	110.9
1946	18.5	26.0	20.1	−7.5	127.5	113.8
1947	17.3	15.5	5.7	1.8	115.4	100.6
1948	16.8	12.1	3.7	4.8	102.2	87.7
1949	15.0	14.8	5.0	0.2	96.2	81.6
1950	14.8	16.0	5.2	−1.2	96.6	82.4
1951	16.5	14.5	7.5	1.9	81.4	68.4
1952	19.4	19.9	13.5	−0.4	76.1	63.1
1953	19.1	20.9	14.5	−1.8	73.1	60.0
1954	18.9	19.3	13.4	−0.3	73.6	61.0
1955	17.0	17.8	11.1	−0.8	71.3	58.9
1956	17.9	17.0	10.2	0.9	65.5	53.4
1957	18.3	17.5	10.4	0.8	62.1	50.0
1958	17.8	18.4	10.4	−0.6	62.4	50.5
1959	16.5	19.2	10.2	−2.7	59.9	48.9
1960	18.3	18.3	9.5	0.1	57.6	46.9
1961	18.3	18.9	9.6	−0.6	56.6	46.1
1962	18.0	19.2	9.4	−1.3	54.6	44.7
1963	18.2	19.0	9.1	−0.8	53.1	43.5
1964	18.0	19.0	8.8	−0.9	50.5	41.1
1965	17.4	17.6	7.5	−0.2	48.0	38.9
1966	17.8	18.3	7.9	−0.5	44.7	35.9
1967	18.8	19.8	9.0	−1.1	42.9	33.6
1968	18.1	21.0	9.7	−3.0	43.5	34.2
1969	20.2	19.8	8.9	0.4	39.5	30.0
1970	19.6	19.9	8.3	−0.3	38.7	28.7
1971	17.8	20.0	7.5	−2.2	38.8	28.8
1972	18.1	20.1	6.9	−2.0	38.0	28.1
1973	18.1	19.3	6.0	−1.2	36.6	26.8
1974	18.8	19.2	5.7	−0.4	34.5	24.5
1975	18.5	22.0	5.7	−3.5	35.9	26.1
1976	17.7	22.1	5.3	−4.4	37.3	28.3
Transition quarter	18.3	21.6	5.0	−3.3	36.2	27.8
1977	18.5	21.3	5.1	−2.8	36.8	28.6
1978	18.5	21.3	4.8	−2.7	36.0	28.2
1979	19.1	20.7	4.8	−1.7	34.1	26.3
1980	19.6	22.3	5.1	−2.8	34.4	26.8
1981	20.2	22.9	5.3	−2.7	33.5	26.5
1982	19.8	23.9	5.9	−4.1	36.4	29.4
1983	18.1	24.4	6.3	−6.3	41.3	34.1

(continued)

Table 3.2 **(Continued)**

| Fiscal Year | Receipts | Outlays | | Surplus or Deficit (−) | Gross Federal Debt (end of period) | |
		Total	National Defense		Total	Held by Public
1984	18.0	23.1	6.2	−5.0	42.3	35.2
1985	18.5	23.9	6.4	−5.4	45.8	37.8
1986	18.2	23.5	6.5	−5.2	50.3	41.2
1987	19.2	22.5	6.3	−3.4	52.7	42.4
1988	18.9	22.1	6.0	−3.2	54.1	42.6
1989	19.2	22.1	5.9	−2.9	55.4	42.3
1990	18.8	22.9	5.5	−4.0	58.5	44.0
1991	18.6	23.3	4.8	−4.8	63.4	47.4
1992	18.4	23.3	5.0	−4.9	67.4	50.5
1993	18.3	22.4	4.6	−4.0	69.1	51.6
1994[1]	18.8	22.3	4.2	−3.5	70.4	52.3
1995[1]	19.1	21.6	3.9	−2.5	70.6	51.9

[1]Estimates.
Source: U.S. Office of Management and Budget.

Figure 3.4 **Medicare and Medicaid Expenditures, 1970–1993**

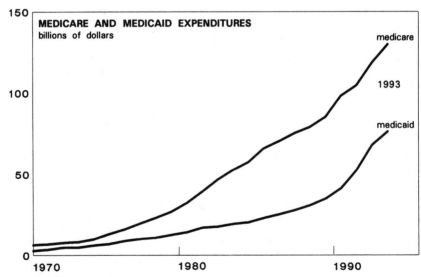

Source: Congressional Budget Office.

is held by the public.) The annual interest payments to the public on this mountain of debt have escalated to more than $200 billion (see Figure 3.5). This is now such a large outlay that it has tended to elbow out other more socially desirable expenditures.

Renewed efforts at deficit reduction would not only trim the government's interest outlays and make way for more beneficial expenditures, but they also would foster a better environment for your investments. If you see more substantive spending restraints that produce declines in the ratio of the deficit to GDP, then you'll know that the government's attempts to cut the deficit are effective. It is hoped that these deficit-cutting efforts will exert additional downward pressure on long-term interest rates in the future, or at least limit the extent to which long-term interest rates might rise in periods of strengthening economic activity as investors regain their faith in the government's fiscal discipline.

A general rule for what you and your fellow individual investors should watch for in seeking to determine if government deficit-cutting efforts might have some future impact on your bond and stock holdings is whether government constraints on expenditures reduce the rate of growth of spending substantially below the

Figure 3.5   **Interest Payments to the Public, 1970–1993**

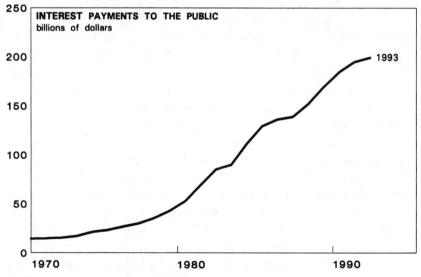

Source: U.S. Office of Management and Budget.

rate of growth in the tax base (GDP). In addition, you should determine whether the administration in power is willing to propose tax increases as a last resort if spending restraint proves to be inadequate. Ideally, the government will offer believable spending and tax policies that place the ratio of the deficit to GDP on a prolonged downward path that persists for more than five years.

DEFICIT-CUTTING LEGISLATION

As the budget deficit problem threatened to get out of hand in the mid-1980s, Congress was finally motivated to try to take action. There was a whiff of fiscal restraint in the air with the passage of the Gramm-Rudman law in December 1985, but it was perhaps the most bizarre piece of budget legislation ever passed. The cumbersome and convoluted deficit-cutting machinery in this unusual law revealed the reluctance of Congress to set budget priorities and limit the growth in total outlays. It set in place the provision that if the President and Congress could not agree on the required annual deficit-cutting steps, then certain across-the-board spending cuts would take place in order to achieve the budget-balancing objectives. The precise size of the deficit and therefore the "automatic" spending cuts were to be determined by the General Accounting Office (GAO), Congress's financial watchdog, based on information from the Congressional Budget Office (CBO) and the administration's Office of Management and Budget (OMB). The Gramm-Rudman law sought initially to balance the budget by 1991 (see Table 3.3).

As predicted, the Gramm-Rudman plan ran afoul of the Supreme Court, which declared it unconstitutional on the grounds of its delegation of power over budget matters from the Executive Branch to Congress. In September 1987, Congress enacted a Gramm-Rudman budget law revision which met the Supreme Court's legal objections by putting the "automatic" deficit-cutting machinery in the hands of the executive branch's OMB, rather than Congress's GAO. However, this revision dealt a blow to fiscal credibility by extending the target for balancing the budget to 1993. Subsequently, the October 1987 stock market crash prodded the White House and congressional leaders to hold a Budget Summit and agree on special deficit-cutting measures for fiscal years 1988

Table 3.3 **Gramm-Rudman Deficit Projections versus Reality, Fiscal 1986–1993**
(Billions of Dollars)

Fiscal Year	Original Law	1987 Revision	Actual Deficit
1986	171.9	—	221.2
1987	144.0	—	149.8
1988	108.0	144.0	155.2
1989	72.0	136.0	152.5
1990	36.0	100.0	221.4
1991	-0-	64.0	269.5
1992	—	28.0	290.4
1993	—	-0-	254.7

Source: Gramm-Rudman deficit-cutting law and U.S. Office of Management and the Budget.

and 1989; despite these good intentions, domestic and foreign investors alike found the Budget Summit measures ineffective, since they did little to curb runaway government entitlement programs or to raise significant amounts of tax revenue.

In October 1990, the Republican Bush administration and a hostile Democrat-controlled Congress finally hammered out a deficit-cutting act with teeth in it. President Bush broke his "read my lips" promise not to raise taxes (an act that probably cost him his reelection), proposed deep defense-spending cuts, and placed some extremely tough limits on discretionary spending. The Clinton administration followed with a 1993 deficit-cutting package, which passed the Senate by one vote. This package reinforced discretionary spending discipline, made deeper cuts in defense spending, and raised taxes, primarily on the wealthy, by a considerable amount.

The Bush and Clinton administrations' combined deficit-cutting measures turned the corner in the direction of fiscal discipline. Investors at long last seemed to believe that U.S. deficits could be reined in and kept in control relative to the economy's longer-term capacity to service the debt through increased revenues. Their renewed faith was reflected in a huge drop in the budget deficit to approximately $200 billion in fiscal 1994 (well below government estimates) from about $255 billion in fiscal 1993. This remarkable deficit decline reflected rising recovery-induced revenues, declining defense spending, and caps on discretionary spending. The ratio of the federal deficit to GDP is projected to be about cut in half by 1995 from 4.9% as recently as 1992 (see Table 3.2).

WATCHING THE GLOBAL DEFICIT

If you invest in global mutual funds that include foreign sovereign bonds in their portfolios, then you must keep an eye not only on capital flows, currency fluctuations, political risk, and commitment to free markets but also on budget issues in foreign countries in which you are investing. This is because a country's fiscal and monetary policy discipline is crucial to its access to global financial markets to help finance its economic growth. At present, there appear to be only about 20 major countries that have complete access to global financial markets for both their public and private sectors. To reach this hallowed status, a country must have believable budget-spending limits, including effective limitations on government subsidies and entitlements. Also, the government should be pursuing the privatization of government functions such as transportation that can be performed more efficiently in the private sector. If adequate spending discipline can be achieved, this should be evident in well-behaved debt measures. For example, the ratio of government debt to GDP should be on a prolonged downward glide path. Under the Maastricht Treaty of European unification approved in 1991, each of the 12 European Union (EU) countries were encouraged to hold their ratios of total government debt to GDP under 60%. Moreover, for each country the ratio of annual government deficits to GDP should remain below the level of 3%, the upper limit for each country's deficit/GDP ratio established in the Maastricht Treaty.

In order to keep an eye on capital flows, current account trade deficits and budget policies, you can subscribe to the International Monetary Fund (IMF) *Survey of International Statistics*. For more current data on exchange rate fluctuations and political developments in the major industrial economies, you should read the international section of the daily *Wall Street Journal* or published research reports by major commercial banks like J. P. Morgan or investment banks with a significant international business like Goldman Sachs. Of course, by investing in any well-regarded global mutual fund you will gain access to its extensive research capabilities. Nevertheless, you should examine the specific foreign holdings of your global fund periodically to be sure that its investments have not become excessively concentrated in the debt of one or two countries that happen to be following imprudent fiscal or monetary policies.

As the United States seeks to reduce its deficit sharply as a percentage of GDP, many of the 12 major European Union countries appear to be moving in the opposite direction. The deteriorating budget problems in EU countries partly reflect slumping revenue growth as a result of widespread recessionary conditions and partly reveal deeper and more intractable structural problems. Most EU countries have extensive social safety nets and worker compensation programs that are paid for by tax revenues exceeding 50% of GDP. Also, the cost of labor is relatively high. The average hourly wages and benefits for German auto workers are $26, compared to a much smaller $16 for U.S. auto workers. Meanwhile, they face competition from such newly industrial economies (NIEs) as Hong Kong and Singapore that have cheap labor and extremely limited social safety nets. (They say a worker's own family should be the social safety net.) The bottom line is that the post–Cold War world is lunging toward competitive free market conditions in which a large pool of global capital relentlessly seeks out the highest return and tends to serve as a major disciplining force on a country's fiscal and monetary policies.

Next year, you should be on guard as increasing EU government-borrowing demands clash with gradually increasing private investment needs as the EU countries begin to recover. These competing demands among governments, industry, and individuals will press heavily on a limited availability of savings, exerting upward pressure on real long-term interest rates. As a result, you can expect that because of rising interest rates on European bonds, your mutual funds holding these obligations will suffer near-term capital losses, thus trimming total returns on global bond funds. The best bet would be for you to retreat to heavier cash positions until European bond rates reach higher levels.

In terms of any foreign investment, always focus on whether the host country has long-term fiscal credibility. One clue to such commitment is its level of political stability. Most countries that have excessive political instability will also lack fiscal credibility. One present exception is Japan, which has considerable political instability, having just formed its fourth new government in little more than a year. Even so, Japan retains its longer-term fiscal credibility, because entrenched bureaucracies like the Ministry of Finance have the dominant influence on fiscal policy.

In sum, you can't ignore the impact of budget policies on either your domestic or international bond funds. Fiscal policies will typically have a significant impact on long-term interest rates. For example, upward pressure is likely to be exerted on long-term interest rates when budget-spending discipline is lacking and there is the threat that a prolonged rise in budget deficits will outpace the rate of increase in a country's tax base (GDP). This condition would be reflected in a prolonged rise in the ratio of the deficit to GDP.

Of course, the precise impact of budget policies on long-term interest rates will depend on other factors such as fluctuations in the foreign exchange value of the dollar, and especially investor inflationary expectations. For instance, in cases when the foreign exchange value of the dollar is falling and investor inflation expectations are rising, there is likely to be significant upward pressure on long-term interest rates. Just the same, there is little question that budget policies can in most cases impact importantly on your bond fund profits, as in 1993 when unexpectedly aggressive Clinton administration deficit-cutting measures contributed importantly to the spectacular bond market rally.

4

Using Federal Reserve Policy to Guide Investments

Whenever you feel that you might be thrown off balance by large financial market waves, remember that the Federal Reserve is your best compass to safe passage through these troubled waters. This chapter will show that it's up to you to determine whether the Fed is a friend or foe of your investing. If you follow this book's suggestions and keep an eye trained on the Fed, it can provide a beacon that guides your portfolio to a safe port. If not, Fed policy shifts can sink your investments in the depths of the stormy seas.

To be sure, you might think that it's not easy to figure out the Fed. After all, isn't the Fed a secretive body that creates new money out of thin air without warning? "How" you might ask, "can I get an inside track on the plans of this secretive body?" This chapter will show you that the Fed is not inscrutable and that your efforts to interpret and anticipate its maneuvers will greatly impact your financial future.

The Fed is the most important and effective governmental policymaking body. It has a more important and direct influence on your investment fortunes than you probably ever imagined. Quite simply, when the Fed takes steps to pump up the availability of credit and lower the cost of borrowing, you almost always can expect big rallies in bonds and stocks to follow. Conversely, when the Fed seeks to curtail the availability of credit and push borrowing costs higher, stocks and bonds will usually go into a slump. Given this powerful influence over the direction of the financial markets, you clearly cannot invest safely or predictably if you don't keep a steady watch on the Fed.

PICTURING THE FED AS THE SUPREME COURT OF FINANCE

To get a handle on the Fed, you could think of it as the Supreme Court of finance. Essentially, the Fed is to financial and economic policy what the Supreme Court is to law. In other words, just as the Supreme Court is the legal authority of last resort, the Fed is the lender and economic policymaker of last resort. In order to command public respect in our representative democracy, both institutions must show continuity, stability, and a measure of predictability in their actions. Ideally, the Fed should consist of experienced, competent, and objective professionals, who rise above partisan politics in making reasoned judgments about the appropriate degree of monetary stimulus or restraint required to achieve sustainable, noninflationary economic growth. If the Fed wants to keep from disrupting the markets needlessly, it has to pursue these noble goals with *credibility*, *consistency*, and *commitment*.

As the "Supreme Court of finance," the Fed can do something that no one else in this country can do: it can create new funds or credit out of thin air. To do this, Fed officials write a check to buy U.S. government securities even though, technically, there aren't funds in the Fed's account to cover the check. In that fashion, more money is put into circulation. So, you might ask, why doesn't the Fed write lots of checks and create an endless amount of new money and credit, and this way, we will all live happily ever after. The problem is that if the Fed creates too much new money and credit, it creates an inflationary condition of increasing prices on the goods and services that we all need to buy. Of course, rising inflation is the cruelest tax of all on our purchasing power.

STRUCTURE OF THE FEDERAL RESERVE

The Federal Reserve System is composed of a Board of Governors, located in Washington, D.C., and 12 district Federal Reserve Banks, located in Boston, New York, Philadelphia, Cleveland,

Richmond, Atlanta, Chicago, St. Louis, Minneapolis, Kansas City, Dallas, and San Francisco. The president of the United States, with the advice and consent of the Senate, appoints the seven members of the Board of Governors to 14-year terms. These long terms were set deliberately to protect them from the changing political climate. The Board leadership, however, has a shorter tenure. The chairman and vice chairman of the Board of Governors are each appointed by the president to hold these titles for four-year terms, renewable at the president's pleasure and with the advice and consent of the Senate.

Each of the 12 district Federal Reserve Banks has a president, who is chosen by its respective Board of Directors, with the approval of the Board of Governors in Washington, D.C. Each Reserve Bank's Board of Directors consists of nine members; six are elected by member banks in each district and three are appointed by the Board of Governors in Washington, D.C.

You might feel that the Federal Reserve System is too unwieldy with a Board in Washington, D.C., and all those Reserve Banks spread around the country. Actually, this structure operates efficiently, particularly when different regions of the nation are growing at varying rates and the regional Reserve Bank officials can highlight these conditions during Fed policy deliberations. Also, the Reserve Bank presidents tend to reinforce Fed independence from undue political pressure since they come from outside the Washington beltway.

THE FED'S POLICY TOOLS

The Fed has two primary policy tools: (1) the discount rate—this is the rate the Fed charges depository institutions for the privilege of borrowing funds at its discount window; it is a largely symbolic tool; and (2) open market operations—this activity consists of purchases (or sales) of government securities for the purpose of increasing (or decreasing) bank reserve availability. Discount rate changes are initiated by the Board of Directors of one or more Reserve Banks, but only the Board of Governors in Washington, D.C., may approve, by majority vote, an actual change in the Federal Reserve discount rate. Open market operations are under the control of the Federal Open Market Committee (FOMC), which is a larger policymaking body consisting of the Board of Governors plus five voting Reserve Bank presidents.

The Federal Reserve Board of Governors has one other tool that is powerful yet infrequently used. From time to time, it uses its authority to adjust reserve requirements that member banks must legally hold against all their transaction accounts. This policy tool would be used when the Fed wants to reinforce a tightening (or easing) action with a high-visibility move that instantly affects all depository institutions. Currently, reserve requirements on bank transaction accounts are roughly 10%, and there are no reserve requirements on bank time deposits. Previously, in an effort to help counter the credit crunch which stifled the economy during the 1990–91 recession, the Federal Reserve Board of Governors lowered reserve requirements in both December 1990 and again in February 1991. This increased the amount of interest-earning loans and investments that banks can hold while simultaneously lowering their nonearning required reserves, thereby potentially improving bank profitability.

THE HEART OF FED POLICY MOVES

The Fed's most important policymaking body is the Federal Open Market Committee. It is in charge of the Fed's most important policy tool—open market operations. The FOMC, which consists of the seven members of the Board of Governors plus five voting Reserve Bank presidents, meets eight times per year in regularly scheduled meetings and, if special unforeseen circumstances should arise, at other times through special telephone conferences.

As an interested investor seeking to identify Fed policy shifts, you will benefit greatly from a major change in the way the Fed reports its official actions. Starting with its initial move to tighten credit availability on February 4, 1994, the monetary authorities have begun to announce policy changes effected through open market operations immediately (see Exhibit 4.1). Moreover, the wording of these immediate announcements of policy shifts gives an important clue to the magnitude of the change in the overnight federal funds rate that is associated with the Fed's easing or tightening action. For example, in the Fed's actions to tighten the supply of credit on February 4, March 22, and April 18 of 1994, the magni-

Exhibit 4.1 Official Statements of FOMC Actions

Friday, February 4, 1994 at 11:05 A.M.—FOMC Meeting

"Chairman Alan Greenspan announced today that the Federal Open Market Committee decided to increase *slightly* the degree of pressure on reserve positions. The action is expected to be associated with a *small* increase in short-term money market interest rates.

"The decision was taken to move toward a less accommodative stance in monetary policy in order to sustain and enhance the economic expansion.

"Chairman Greenspan decided to announce this action immediately so as to avoid any misunderstanding of the committee's purposes, given the fact that this is the first firming of reserve market conditions by the committee since early 1989."

Tuesday, March 22, 1994 at 2:20 P.M.—FOMC Meeting

"Chairman Alan Greenspan announced today that the Federal Open Market Committee decided to increase *slightly* the degree of pressure on reserve positions. This action is expected to be associated with a *small* increase in short-term money market interest rates."

Monday, April 18, 1994 at 10:06 A.M.—FOMC Telephone Conference Call

"Chairman Alan Greenspan announced today that the Federal Reserve will increase *slightly* the degree of pressure on reserve positions. This action is expected to be associated with a *small* increase in short-term money market interest rates."

Tuesday, May 17, 1994 at 2:26 P.M.—FOMC Meeting

"The Federal Reserve today announced two actions designed to maintain favorable trends in inflation and thereby sustain the economic expansion.

"The Board approved an increase in the discount rate from 3 percent to $3^1/_2$ percent, effective immediately, and the Federal Open Market Committee agreed that this increase should be allowed to show through completely into interest rates in reserve markets.

"These actions, combined with the three adjustments initiated earlier this year by the FOMC, substantially remove the degree of monetary accommodation which prevailed throughout 1993. As always, the Federal Reserve will continue to monitor economic and financial developments to judge the appropriate stance of monetary policy.

"In taking the discount action, the Board approved requests submitted by the Boards of Directors of eleven Federal Reserve Banks—Boston, New York, Philadelphia, Richmond, Atlanta, Chicago, St. Louis, Minneapolis, Kansas City, Dallas and San Francisco. The discount rate is the interest rate that is charged depository institutions when they borrow from their district Federal Reserve Bank."

Wednesday, July 6, 1994 at 2:18 P.M.—FOMC Meeting

A Fed official said, "the FOMC meeting ended at 12:35 P.M." and the Fed "does not plan to make any further announcements."

Tuesday, August 16, 1994 at 1:18 P.M.—FOMC Meeting

"The Board of Governors approved an increase in the discount rate from 3.5% to 4% effective immediately.

"The Federal Open Market Committee agreed that this increase would be allowed to show through completely into interest rates in reserve markets.

(continued)

Exhibit 4.1   (Continued)

"These measures were taken against the background of evidence of continuing strength in the economic expansion and high levels of resource utilization. The actions are intended to keep inflationary pressures contained, and thereby foster sustainable economic growth.

"The Federal Reserve will continue to monitor economic and financial developments to gauge the appropriate stance of policy. But these actions are expected to be sufficient, at least for a time, to meet the objective of sustained, non-inflationary growth.

"In taking the discount rate action, the Board approved requests submitted by the Boards of Directors of the Federal Reserve Banks of Boston, New York, Richmond, Kansas City, and Dallas. The discount rate is the interest rate that is charged depository in-stutions when they borrow from their district Federal Reserve Banks."

tude of the targeted increase in the federal funds rate was one quarter of one percentage point in each case. In this regard, you can see that the wording in each of these three announcements was exactly the same: " . . . the Federal Open Market Committee decided to increase *slightly* the degree of pressure on reserve positions. The action is expected to be associated with a *small* increase in short-term money market interest rates" (emphasis).

Alternatively, when the Fed decided on bolder actions on both May 17 and August 16 of 1994, consisting of one-half percentage point increases in both the federal funds rate and the discount rate, the wording was changed to: "The Board approved an increase in the discount rate from 3 percent to 3½ percent, effective immediately, and the Federal Open Market Committee agreed that this increase should be allowed to show through completely into interest rates in reserve markets." In this announcement the "Board" refers to the seven-member Board of Governors of the Federal Reserve, which has the authority to adjust the discount rate. In coordination with the Board's discount rate adjustment, the FOMC decides whether the federal funds rate will be allowed to show through *partially* or *completely*. In the May 17 and August 16, 1994 situations the complete "show through" meant that the one-half percentage point increase in the discount rate in each case was associated with a one-half percentage point increase in the federal funds rate; a *partial* "show through" would instead presumably mean that a one-half percentage point increase in the discount rate would be associated with a one-quarter percentage point increase in the federal funds rate.

Under the new system of immediate FOMC announcements (previously FOMC policy changes through open market operations were officially announced with a 5- to 6-week delay; only discount rate adjustments were announced immediately), when the Fed decides on no policy change it will make only a brief official announcement following the FOMC meeting. For example, following the July 5–6, 1994, FOMC meeting at which no policy change was decided upon, a Fed official, stated at 2:18 P.M. that "the FOMC meeting ended at 12:35 P.M." and that the Fed "does not plan to make any further announcements."

The FOMC can take temporary action to increase bank reserves through system repurchase agreements (system RPs) or more permanent action through outright purchases of U.S. government securities. System RPs represent contracts whereby the Fed agrees to purchase U.S. government securities from any of 39 approved primary dealers within a specified period (usually one day) and then to sell these government securities back to the primary dealer for an agreed-upon interest rate. The FOMC uses System RPs to temporarily ease pressure on bank reserve positions and, consequently, expand credit. At times, the FOMC might want to take a milder action to ease pressures on bank reserve positions more slightly. In that case, the FOMC uses customer repurchase agreements (customer RPs). Customer RPs reduce the drain on bank reserves that would otherwise have occurred if these customer funds had been instead invested internally at the Fed through reverse RPs.

Conversely, the FOMC may act to tighten pressures on bank reserve positions. They can do this temporarily through reverse RPs (otherwise known as matched sale-purchase agreements). In a reverse RP, the Fed sells U.S. government securities temporarily in order to reduce reserve availability. This is typically done to counter the impact of market factors such as float and Treasury deposits at the Fed.

For you to gain insight into Fed policy deliberations with a view to anticipating the next credit tightening (or easing) action, you need to be a regular reader of two important official documents. The *Record of Policy Actions* of the FOMC, which is released 5–6 weeks after each of the eight regularly scheduled FOMC meetings each year, is a comprehensive Fed review of financial and economic conditions, inflationary pressures, and foreign developments. Policy options and goals, intermediate policy indicators and the rationale for any Fed policy shifts are examined in this document. In addition, you should read carefully the semiannual

Humphrey-Hawkins testimony to Congress by the Fed chairman in February and July of each year. This widely publicized Humphrey-Hawkins testimony gives special insight into the main Fed policy concerns, such as the need to curtail future inflationary pressures and what the monetary authorities intend to do about them. (You can obtain each of these important documents by writing to the public information department of the Board of Governors of the Federal Reserve.)

To Figure Out the Fed, You Need to Know About Its Primary Objective

What is the Fed trying to accomplish? The Fed's primary objective is stable prices, because stable prices are a prerequisite to sustainable, long-term economic growth. To that end Fed policymakers are continuously taking the economy's temperature and trying to diagnose any problems so that it can make any adjustments needed to restore economic health. In formulating monetary policy, Fed authorities are partly responding to unforeseen developments and partly trying to anticipate future trends. When, for example, real economic growth appears excessive and there is a threat of accelerating inflationary pressures, the monetary authorities will constrict the money supply by tightening bank reserve pressures and pushing the overnight federal funds rate and other short-term interest rates higher. As former Fed Chairman William McChesney Martin, Jr., was fond of saying, this is akin to taking away the punch bowl before the party gets too wild.

Usually, these Fed-tightening actions will push short-term interest rates up more than long-term interest rates (see Figure 4.1). Note that this was particularly the case in the Fed's credit-tightening actions in 1980, 1981–82, and 1988–89. In these circumstances, you should lighten up on your bond and stock holdings and increase your position in short-term investments whose returns increase in yield in lock-step with Fed-tightening actions.

As short-term rates rise more sharply than long-term rates, in response to Fed actions to tighten up on the availability of credit, bank net interest margins will be squeezed, thereby reducing the banks' incentives to lend to individual and business borrowers. With funds becoming scarcer and more costly, individuals and

Figure 4.1   **Fed Funds Rate and 30-Year Treasury Bond Rate**

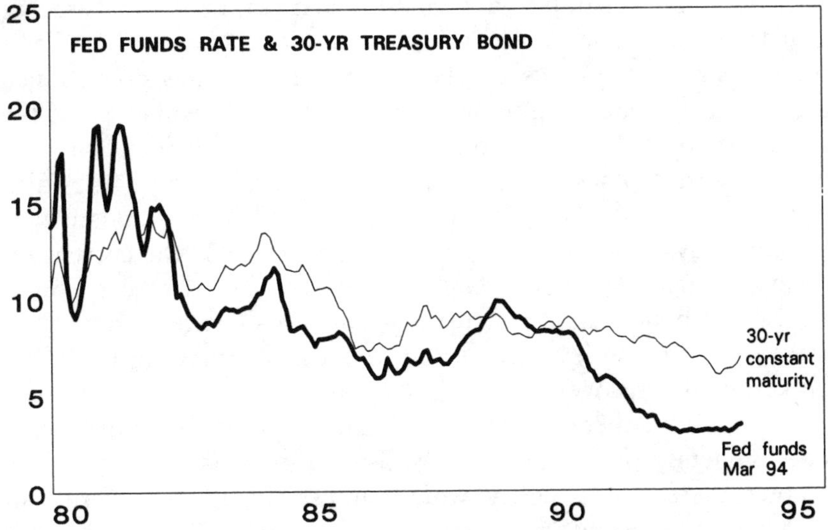

FED FUNDS RATE & 30-YR TREASURY BOND

30-yr
constant
maturity

Fed funds
Mar 94

Source: Federal Reserve.

businesses will curtail borrowing and spending and economic activity will slow, eventually resulting in a reduction in price pressures. A good example of successful Fed-tightening efforts was in the 1979–81 period, when the Volcker Fed broke the back of rampant inflation and conquered lofty inflationary expectations, though at the cost of two back-to-back recessions.

The Fed's attempts to tighten credit do not always push short-term rates up more sharply than long-term rates. In some instances, bond market participants may perceive that Fed policymakers are not tightening vigorously enough to contain inflationary pressures. In that case, long-term rates may rise more sharply than short-term rates.

If real economic growth is turning sluggish and there is a threat of recession, Fed policymakers will respond by increasing the availability of credit and pushing the federal funds rate and other short-term interest rates lower. These easing actions will typically push short-term interest rates down more sharply than long-term interest rates, thereby steepening the yield curve, increasing bank net interest margins, and increasing bank incentives to lend to individual and business borrowers. With money and credit becoming more abundant and cheaper, individuals and businesses will be induced to borrow and spend more, thereby speeding up economic activity. A fine example of successful Fed actions to expand the availability of credit came during the 1989–92 period. The Fed's credit-easing actions pushed short-term interest rates down much more sharply than long-term interest rates. This widening of the spread between short- and long-term interest rates helped bring the banking system back to financial health. Lower interest rates also triggered multiple rounds of much needed debt refinancings, thereby providing a strong financial foundation for the current recovery, though at a cost of massive leveraged global speculation in stocks and bonds. As a result, the decline in short-term rates relative to the drop in long-term rates provides a promising backdrop for sustainable recoveries.

Of course, there are other government policy instruments besides monetary policy. Specifically, as we discussed in the previous chapter, there is fiscal policy, which can use tax cuts or government spending increases to stimulate economic activity. But fiscal policy is cumbersome, and its aim is less certain, as, for example, when anti-recession government spending increases are delayed by political bickering and don't go into effect until the subsequent recovery is well under way, thus potentially adding to inflationary pressures. Often proposals for anti-recession tax cuts or spending increases get bogged down in partisan political squabbling. In addition, trade policy can also influence economic growth: free trade will stimulate growth, while protectionism will stifle growth. But trade policy also suffers the fate of partisan political bickering, and progress toward the ideal objective of free trade is slow and uneven. Thus, monetary policy takes the prize as the government's most flexible and effective policy instrument.

FED-TIGHTENING ACTIONS AND YOUR MONEY

To find dramatic evidence of the power the Fed has over your personal fortunes, you need search no further than February 4, 1994. On that day, the Fed took actions to tighten up the availability of credit. This Fed-tightening step, the first one in five years, was followed by additional moves on March 22, April 18, May 17, and August 16, 1994, and more such steps are likely to be forthcoming given our unexpectedly strong economic growth and the threat of a moderate acceleration in inflation. The Fed tightened aggressively on May 17, and August 16, 1994, increasing both the federal funds and discount rates. In their May 17 effort, Fed officials stated that their tightening actions, combined with the three earlier ones, had "substantially removed the degree of monetary accommodation." In other words, the Fed's easy credit conditions have come to an end and rallies in the stock and bond markets like those in 1993 will be less likely to occur. In their August 16, 1994, actions, Fed policymakers began what is likely to a series of credit-tightening steps aimed at actually restraining economic activity and limiting the threatened acceleration in inflationary pressures.

These Fed-tightening steps jolted the financial markets in the United States and all around the globe. They signaled to the domestic and foreign financial markets alike that the conditions of abundant liquidity were coming to an end. As a result, there was the sudden and shocking unwinding of leveraged speculative positions in stocks and bonds around the world. This massive sell-off of assets brought your soaring bond and stock mutual funds down to earth very hard and very fast.

The nose dive that your stock mutual fund was thrust into by the Fed's February 4, 1994, tightening move is evident in Table 4.1. Up until February 3, 1994, the day before the Fed's tightening action, your stock funds were sailing along nicely. Among the big gainers both in the preceding 12 months and in 1994 until the Fed's initial credit-tightening step were such stock mutual fund categories as global small company, international, Latin American, European region, science and technology, gold, emerging markets, health/biotechnology and Japanese. In contrast, following the Fed's February 4 tightening step, there were virtual across-the-board declines in total return on your equity mutual funds. These drops range from the smallest decline of 0.7% for real estate funds to the largest decline of 13.66% for Latin American stock mutual funds. It should be noted that the political fears associated with the assassination of the ruling party presidential candidate in Mexico contributed, along with the Fed-tightening move, to the plunge in Latin American funds. The only exception to the across-the-board plunge prompted by the Fed's February tightening step was the Japanese fund, which actually rose 4.91% as hopes for a Japanese recovery intensified.

The post-February 4 trauma was, to the dismay of Clinton ad-

Table 4.1 Mutual Fund Performance, First Quarter 1994

Mutual-fund returns in the first month of the quarter far exceeded returns during February and March, after the Fed had raised interest rates.

Fund Category	Total Return				Fund Category	Total Return			
	Qtr 1	12 Months	Feb. 3, 1994	Rest of Qtr		Qtr 1	12 Months	Feb. 3, 1994	Rest of Qtr
Japanese	17.26%	24.00%	11.74%	4.91%	Capital Appreciation	-3.40%	8.34%	3.44%	-6.60%
Science and Technology	1.27	21.23	5.26	-4.13	Growth	-3.44	3.79	3.23	-6.47
European Region	1.09	21.36	6.46	-5.06	Natural Resources	-3.55	4.79	6.69	-9.65
Real Estate	0.81	5.77	1.86	-0.70	Equity Income	-3.75	2.78	2.75	-6.32
Global Small Company	-0.37	25.49	5.70	-5.75	Environmental	-4.31	-2.23	5.79	-10.02
International	-1.00	24.75	6.48	-7.00	Health/Biotech	-4.44	14.36	5.11	-9.11
Global	-2.41	19.32	5.24	-7.20	Gold	-4.75	40.05	2.29	-6.71
Latin American	-2.65	47.24	12.72	-13.64	Utility	-6.87	-2.53	-0.34	-6.46
Canadian	-2.88	16.14	4.21	-6.78	Emerging Markets	-7.51	45.07	5.19	-11.97
Small Company	-2.99	11.13	2.93	-5.69	Pacific Region	-11.51	33.08	0.82	-12.49
Financial Services	-2.99	0.21	2.81	-5.66	Average Stock Fund	-3.33	5.43	3.14	-6.25
Growth and Income	-3.18	3.31	3.15	-6.13	Standard & Poor's 500 (w/dividends)	-3.79	1.46	N.A.	N.A.
Mid-Cap	-3.20	10.80	2.86	-5.91					

[1]Through March 31, 1994.
N.A. – Not available.

ministration officials, no less severe in the long-term maturity sector of the bond market. Shockingly, the yield on 30-year Treasury bonds soared to 7.43% on April 4, 1994, from 6.23% on January 28, 1994. Actually, tax-free muni bond funds suffered the largest drop in total returns, followed by intermediate munis, corporate A-rated bond funds, and U.S. government bond funds.

It is important to note that the surge in long-term rates did not stem entirely from the Fed's move. Also exerting upward pressure on bond rates was unexpectedly strong real economic growth (reflected in a nearly 7% jump in GDP in the final quarter of 1993) and the accompanying fears of higher inflation. Also, there was the February 11 breakdown in trade negotiations between the United States and Japan, threatening a protectionist trade war. In response, the dollar plunged and foreign investors fearing that the Clinton administration might talk the dollar lower, dumped dollar-denominated bonds. In addition, mounting tensions between the United States and North Korea resulted in concern that the Clinton administration could not cut defense spending as much as anticipated, thus lessening progress in cutting the deficit and exerting upward pressure on long-term interest rates. And, finally, there was the abrupt global unwinding of large, leveraged speculative holdings in bonds, as well as equities, and also technical problems with suddenly illiquid dealer holdings of mortgage-backed securities. All these factors boosted bond yields, and yet the Fed's action was the catalyst behind this abrupt and severe change in our financial fortunes. Eventually, investors took heart from the Fed's decisive and well-explained May 17 and August 16, 1994, tightening actions, and both bonds and stocks responded by initially rallying strongly in each case.

INVESTOR RULES FOR FED WATCHING

When the Fed begins a series of tightening steps, such as its February 4, 1994, move, you would do well to keep in mind some simple rules.

Rule 1: Don't panic when the Fed tightens up on the availability of credit. Instead, you should deliberately and rationally move to adjust your investments. For example, the economic recovery may be in its advanced stages with high (85%) and rising capacity utilization rates and low (6%) and falling unemployment rates. If the Fed responds with three or more consecutive tightening steps to restrain the supply of credit, you should sell all your holdings of long-term bonds and then invest half the proceeds in 2- to 5-year Treasury securities and half in short-term money market investments such as 3- to 6-month Treasury bills. The reason you should sell all your bonds is because of the likelihood of capital losses with increased volatility and rising interest rates (see Table 4.2). The reason you should split the proceeds from your bond sales equally between, say, 3-month Treasury bills and 5-year Treasury notes is because the bills are safe and their rates move up in lock-step with Fed credit-tightening action, while the yield on 5-year notes is attractive, usually capturing 75–85% of the yield on 30-year bonds but with only 50% of the volatility.

Rule 2: Pay close attention to the remarks of the Fed chairman when policy shifts are imminent. Specifically, the Fed chairman might refer to the threat of increasing inflationary pressures, excessively high economic growth, strains on productive capacity, or labor shortages.

If a Fed-induced interest rate shift is in motion, listen also to statements by Fed policymakers for clues about subsequent Fed moves. For example, *The New York Times* (April 8, 1994) stated

Table 4.2 **Bond Market Blues, First Quarter**
How several major categories of bond mutual funds have been caught in the bond market debacle.

	Total Return		
	March 94	First Quarter	12 Months[1]
Tax-free bond funds			
General municipals	−4.38%	−5.86%	1.86%
Intermediate municipals	−2.84	−3.95	2.93
Short-term municipals	−1.14	−1.46	2.61
General taxable funds			
General U.S. government	−2.43	−3.17	1.63
Intermediate U.S. government	−1.99	−2.68	1.68
Short-term U.S. government	−1.03	−1.19	1.90
Corporate funds A-rated	−2.63	−3.35	2.47
Intermediate investment-grade corporate	−2.18	−2.71	2.30
Short-term investment-grade corporate	−0.83	−0.81	2.69

[1]Through March 31, 1994.
Source: Lipper Analytical Services, Inc. Reprinted by permission of the *Wall Street Journal*
© 1994 Dow-Jones & Company, Inc. All rights reserved worldwide.

in its bond column that Fed Governor Lawrence B. Lindsey had observed that labor market slack was "diminishing." In this same article, there was reference to another Fed official, Silas Keehn, president of the Chicago Federal Reserve Bank, who warned that some areas of the manufacturing sector were approaching full capacity. Obviously, these statements by Fed officials reflected worries about future wage and price pressures, which are important grounds for future Fed-tightening actions. Indeed, the Fed tightened credit promptly thereafter on April 18. Subsequently, more Fed credit-tightening moves came on May 17, and August 16, 1994, and still more are in the cards. Aside from the newspapers, you can follow the commentary of the Fed chairman by reading Federal Reserve press releases. You might write to the Public Information Department of the Federal Reserve Board of Governors in Washington, D.C., and have your name put on the mailing list for the Fed chairman's statements.

Rule 3: Watch what the Fed actually watches, not what you think the Fed should watch. These are four different sources of information that you need to review in order to follow this rule: (1) FOMC minutes, (2) congressional testimony, (3) the beige book, and (4) the lending practices survey. You should read the FOMC minutes and congressional testimony of Fed officials to find the main inflation indicators Fed policymakers are tracking. In the minutes for the November 16, 1993, FOMC meeting, for instance, your search would have hit pay dirt. Specifically, you would have found the statement that ". . . a number of [FOMC] members observed that at this point they did not see the usual indications of any near-term intensification of inflationary pressures such as general increases in commodity prices, lengthening delivery lead times along with efforts to increase inventories, and strong growth of credit." Clearly, you could use this list of early signals of inflationary pressures to help anticipate Fed-tightening moves. As noted, you can obtain this information by writing to the Public Information Department of the Board of Governors of the Federal Reserve.

The Fed's beige book of regional economic developments is key during periods when the Fed is beginning to worry about strong economic growth and potential inflationary pressures. Scrutinize it to see if there is any mention of scattered shortages of skilled labor or of some firms pushing up against capacity constraints. "Scattered labor shortages" were noted in the Fed's January 1994 beige book. "Strong demand and scattered capacity constraints" were noted in some Fed districts in the Fed's February 1994 beige book. And the Fed's April 1994 beige book noted that production of autos, vehicle parts, steel, and building materials is near capacity. The beige book is usually well reported in *The Wall Street Journal*, or you can obtain it by writing to the Public Information Department of your district Federal Reserve Bank.

Review the lending practices survey published by the Federal Reserve for a look at strengthening credit growth as an early signal of price pressures. Put your name on the Fed Board of Governors' mailing list for the quarterly *Senior Loan Officer Opinion Survey on Bank Lending Practices*. This quarterly survey reviews current bank-lending habits. The January 1994 edition stated that banks reported an easing in terms and standards on business loans to firms of all sizes. Banks also reported an increased willingness to make loans to individuals along with "a small net easing" of credit standards on home mortgages. Also, this same edition noted that a significant number of banks reported an increase in credit *demand* over the preceding three months. Of course, you can also evaluate bank credit growth by means of weekly figures on commercial bank business loans, loans to individuals and real estate loans, also provided by the Federal Reserve. To obtain this information, write to the Public Information Department of the Board of Governors of the Federal Reserve and ask for the release.

Rule 4: Remember that perhaps your best clue to an impending Fed policy shift is when actual economic activity turns out significantly different from Fed policymakers' expectations. This rule was illustrated in the final quarter of 1993 when the initially estimated real GDP growth soared by 7.5%, well above the Fed's earlier estimates. (This fourth quarter 1993 real GDP growth rate estimate was subsequently revised down to a still hefty 6.3%.) Against the background of relatively lean inventories, businesses have recently had difficulty maintaining sufficient stock on their shelves to meet demand. Fed officials are undoubtedly aware that deliberate business efforts to rebuild their inventory stocks could result in sharp increases in production, employment, and income in the months ahead. Similarly, Fed officials are undoubtedly impressed by the sizable increases supplier delivery lead times and nonfarm payroll employment in April 1994.

As the role of the banking system as a source of credit declines in importance, the Fed may have more difficulty determining how much it needs to tighten credit availability (or ease it) to have the desired effect on economic activity. Therefore, while Fed credit-tightening actions can still operate to curtail inflationary pressures and conversely Fed credit-easing steps can still help boost a slumping economy, the burden on the Fed is to determine how much it needs to do in each case to get the job done.

In this connection, certain capital market innovations in the area of mortgage finance have recently served to complicate the Fed's effort to determine how much it should adjust its policy stance to have the desired impact on economic activity. Specifically, according to a recently released Federal Reserve Bank of New York study, the growing importance of the mortgage-backed securities market (see Chapter 10) accelerated changes in long-term rates, in response to the Fed's credit-tightening steps that boosted short-term interest rates in the spring of 1994. For you as an individual investor, this means that the volatility of your bond mutual funds will be all the greater in response to Fed credit-tightening measures. This should give you all the more incentive to follow the central theme of this book, which is that you should key your major portfolio adjustments to Fed policy shifts. In this case, in response to three or more consecutive Fed-tightening steps within a year, you should avoid major capital losses on your bond holdings by selling them and investing the proceeds in short-term investments.

FOLLOWING REAL SHORT-TERM RATES

In his July 1993 Humphrey-Hawkins congressional testimony, Fed Chairman Greenspan introduced a new policy approach that centers on real short-term interest rates and acknowledges the "crucial" role of expectations in the inflation process. Fed Chairman Greenspan observed that "even expectations not validated by economic fundamentals can themselves add appreciably to wage and price pressures for a considerable period, potentially derailing the economy from its growth track." He added that "inflation expectations and price pressures, unless contained, could raise long-term interest rates and stall economic expansion."

You can get a ballpark approximation of real short-term rates

Figure 4.2   **Real Short-Term Interest Rates, 1975–1994. Fed funds rate minus year-over-year percentage change in CPI percent.**

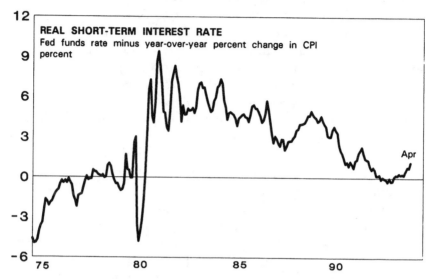

Source: Aubrey G. Lanston & Co., Inc.

if you look at the federal funds rate less inflation expectations. Of course, the crucial element of "inflation expectations" is not directly measurable, but for the purposes of a rough estimate, you can use the FOMC's annual forecast for consumer prices as an approximation of inflation expectations. For example, in 1994 the FOMC forecast a consumer price increase of "about 3%" while the federal funds rate was 4¼% as of June 1994. Therefore, as of the middle of 1994, we were looking at real short-term rates of 1¼% (see Figure 4.2).

Preceding the February tightening step, in his Joint Economic Committee congressional testimony Fed Chairman Greenspan had warned that "short-term interest rates are currently abnormally low in real terms." He went on to state that "at some point, absent an unexpected and prolonged weakening of economic activity, we will need to move them to a more neutral stance." Presumably, Chairman Greenspan would view a "neutral" policy stance as one that neither stimulates nor depresses economic activity. In that case, Greenspan might achieve a more neutral stance through increasing real short-term interest rates from a "quite accommodative" level of 0 to perhaps 1–1½%. Under present circumstances that might be considered "neutral," although the postwar norm for the real short-term interest rate in the middle of an economic expansion is 1½–2%.

To accomplish this policy shift from an "accommodative" policy stance to a "neutral" posture, the Fed took four measured steps in the first half of 1994 to increase its target for the nominal Federal funds rate to 4¼% from 3% at the end of 1993. On February 4, 1994, the Fed initially increased its federal funds rate target to 3¼% from 3%. The Fed hiked its federal funds rate target further to 3½% on March 22, and then pushed it still higher to 3¾% on April 18. On May 17, the Fed tightened further, pushing the federal funds rate up to 4¼% from 3¾%. In connection with this tightening move, the Fed also raised the discount rate to 3½% from 3%. By this point, the Fed had reached its interim policy goal of a "neutral" policy stance. Subsequently, on August 16, 1994, the Fed started moving toward a restrictive stance by increasing the discount rate again to 4% from 3½% and increasing the federal funds rate to 4¾% from 4¼%.

Eventually, given continued economic expansion and increased price pressures, Fed Chairman Greenspan and his fellow policymakers will likely find it necessary to raise real short-term interest rates still higher to a more restrictive level, possibly during the rest of 1994 or in 1995. Finding the appropriate restrictive level for real short-term interest rates will unquestionably involve a process of trial and error. So, in the winter of 1994, look for a series of further tightening adjustments, followed by close observations of the resulting economic behavior. By the end of 1994, if the Fed strives for the expected, restrictive real short-term interest rate of 2–2½%, it will have to push its nominal federal funds rate target up to at least 5–5½%, assuming 3% inflation expectations. In the likely event that continued strong economic momentum pushes inflation and inflation expectations higher, still more Fed credit-tightening moves will be required.

The upshot is that you will likely face further Fed credit-tightening actions, meaning that you should follow a defensive investment strategy. You should avoid bonds and invest instead in safe Treasury bills that move up in yield as the Fed tightens and 5-year Treasury notes that provide an attractive yield (presently amounting to about 85% of the 30-year Treasury bond yield), but suffer only about 50% of the volatility or risk of long-term bonds.

Within your stock portfolio you should also follow a more cautious and selective investment approach. Moreover, if Fed credit-tightening actions, perhaps because of undue political pressure, fall behind the appropriate pace required to keep inflationary pressures in check, you should consider shifting 25% of your stock portfolio into real estate, or preferably a diverse natural resource mutual fund with a good track record that will appreciate as inflation expectations rise.

In sum, if you are seeking the maximum amount of return on your investments for the least possible amount of risk, it pays to link your major portfolio shifts to Fed policy actions. To do so you must identify and understand the rationale behind Fed policy shifts. In this way, you might even find it easier to anticipate the next Fed credit-tightening (or easing) action. The bottom line is that a deliberate Fed-oriented investment strategy will be a winning one.

5

Evaluating the Relationship
Between the Chairman
and the President

Your ability to watch the Fed and interpret its actions can only go so far in helping you to protect your finances. You also must understand the personal chemistry and policy relationship between the Fed chairman and the president. Although technically the Fed is supposed to be insulated from each administration's political stance, in reality the Fed chairman's job is highly political.

The Fed is accountable to the public through Congress. This legislative body has the power to implement any desired changes in the structure of the Fed. But Congress has not exercised its legislative influence for the past six decades and effectively has not had a pronounced impact on Fed policy in the ensuing years. Meanwhile, the White House has had a "de facto" influence. Thus, what really counts, both in reality and perception, is the Fed's relationship with the White House.

After all, the seven Federal Reserve governors located in Washington, D.C., are appointed by the president, with the advice and consent of the Senate. Presidential politics are at the center of this process of choosing members of the Board of Governors of the Federal Reserve. Perhaps more important, the chairman and the vice chairman of the Federal Reserve Board of Governors are appointed by the president, with the advice and consent of the Senate, renewable at the president's pleasure. In this selection process the White House will often float names of possible nominees for the chairman's job as trial balloons in order to judge the response of the financial markets.

In order to maintain investors' confidence in the financial markets, it is absolutely essential that the Fed chairman be perceived as independent of undue political pressures. More precisely, while the Fed cannot avoid functioning in a highly charged political environment, investors must believe that it is adhering to a strong anti-inflation stance. Otherwise, domestic and foreign investors will shun our bond market resulting in increased volatility and higher long-term interest rates that could keep the economy from achieving its maximum growth potential. In the final analysis, the Fed must have the leeway to make the objective professional judgments necessary to do its most important job, that of maintaining a sound currency.

To be able to calculate the odds on how effective the Fed is going to be in keeping inflationary pressures in check, and thus how well your stocks and bonds will do, you need to know how the Fed chairman (the second most powerful person in our government) gets along with the most powerful person, the president. Previous chapters have revealed the economic factors that prompt Fed actions. It is not those factors alone, however, that determine Fed policy. You also have to weigh the political variables before you can anticipate, with any accuracy, what the Fed might do next. This chapter will show you how to monitor the political temperature of the relationship between the chairman and the president.

MOTIVES FOR COOPERATION BETWEEN THE PRESIDENT AND THE CHAIRMAN

You would be justified in asking what motivates the two most powerful figures in our government to cooperate: what do they gain, and what do they lose. The Fed chairman runs a Federal Reserve system that is officially an independent agency of Congress. The terms of the seven members of the Board of Governors of the Federal Reserve were deliberately set at a lengthy 14 years, to avoid political interference. While both the White House and Congress can at times exert considerable political pressure on the Fed, the harsh reality is that Fed policymakers have the discretion to exercise at any moment the power to apply enough credit restraint to stop the economy in its tracks. To say the least, this has made presidents wary of the Fed's power, particularly around election time.

It is to be expected that this uneasy relationship between the president and the Fed chairman has produced moments of strain since the Fed's inception in 1913. In the early 1950s, for example, Fed Chairman Marriner Eccles had to fight hard for Fed independence from the Treasury Department's prior edict that the Fed peg interest rates at low levels to help finance World War II. Eccles forcefully argued that the Treasury's edict that the Fed continue to peg interest rates at artificially low levels made the Fed an "engine of inflation." In the mid-1960s, there was another head-on conflict between the Executive Branch and the Fed. In the wake of Johnson administration spending on both the Vietnam war and "Great Society" domestic social programs (guns and butter), Fed Chairman William McChesney Martin, Jr., decided on an anti-inflation move to increase the discount rate. This infuriated President Lyndon Johnson. As a Texas populist, Johnson wanted the Fed instead to make credit more abundant in order to lower its cost and make it easier to obtain for the common people, regardless of the potentially inflationary consequences. Reportedly, in order to try to intimidate Martin into backing down on the discount rate hike, Johnson invited Martin down to the president's Texas ranch and drove him around on dirt roads in a big Lincoln convertible at excessive speeds. Despite the unusual form of presidential intimidation, the Fed chairman did not give in.

In contrast, in today's environment of market deregulation, financial innovation, and completely integrated global financial markets, there is a large pool of mobile capital that relentlessly seeks out countries that generate a high return. Moreover, global investors want these countries to achieve predictable, sustained noninflationary economic growth. In this contemporary setting, instead of trying to intimidate the Fed chairman, the president may be motivated to enlist his support and cooperation so that the president's economic politics will be viewed as credible in the eyes of both domestic and foreign bond investors.

This new approach based on cooperation rather than confrontation was the model for the relationship between President Bill Clinton and Fed Chairman Alan Greenspan. Clinton realized that in order to gain the confidence of bond market investors and facilitate a much needed decline in stubbornly high long-term interest rates, he had to find some common ground of cooperation with the highly respected Fed chairman. From Fed Chairman Greenspan's point of view, he could gain through this cooperation a much needed reduction in the structural budget deficit.

The surprise question in the first presidential debate of the 1992 election year concerned the appropriateness of the Fed's independence in formulating the nation's monetary policies. All three presidential candidates—President George Bush, Democratic challenger Bill Clinton, and brash independent Ross Perot—favored Fed independence from undue partisan political pressures. Interestingly, presidential candidate Bill Clinton was the most outspoken on the need for Fed independence. This strong platform helped form the foundation for an unexpectedly cordial personal relationship between Fed Chairman Alan Greenspan (a true blue Republican) and the Democratic presidential winner.

Actually, the Clinton administration had good reason to keep Alan Greenspan on as Fed chairman. (Greenspan's second term does not expire until March 1996.) Clinton's senior economic advisors saw how the Bush administration's endless public criticism of Greenspan for not easing faster and further to fight the 1990–91 recession was probably counterproductive. An angry Greenspan might not have eased at times because he would have been perceived as caving in to political pressures. Moreover, with Greenspan remaining as Fed chairman, he could help the new administration establish a much needed sense of continuity and credibility. In addition, Clinton greatly desired Greenspan's support in the marketing of his highly complex economic plan—involving contrasting doses of initial fiscal stimulus (later blocked in the Senate) and subsequent restraint in the form of a complex array of deficit-cutting measures.

THE NATIONAL ECONOMIC COUNCIL

One vehicle created by the Clinton administration, through which the White House has stepped up its communications with the Fed, is the new National Economic Council. The most powerful figures in this new body of the Executive Branch are Treasury Secretary Lloyd Bentsen, Secretary of Labor Robert Reich, and Robert Rubin. Former Budget Director Leon Panetta was also a force to be reckoned with on the NEC, though he was subsequently named presidential Chief of Staff, and Alice Rivlin was named his successor. Rubin, the former co-chairman of Wall Street's Goldman Sachs, is the effective head of this council. The president and the members of the National Economic Council meet regularly, and from time to time invite Fed Chairman Greenspan to attend these meetings. This was the case in a highly publicized meeting of this group on March 18, 1994, when Fed Chairman Greenspan abruptly canceled a speech in Houston, Texas, in order to attend. This event stirred intense speculation that the Fed chairman was caving into political pressures not to tighten further. However, this speculation was quickly snuffed out when the Fed tightened soon thereafter on March 22, 1994.

CLINTON'S COURTSHIP OF GREENSPAN

In order to examine the relationship between the Fed chairman and the president, there are some necessary factors to keep in mind. First, you should determine how competent and conservative the president's top economic advisors might prove to be. In President Bill Clinton's case, his surprisingly conservative and competent top economic team included Treasury Secretary Lloyd Bentsen, Leon Panetta, head of the Office of Management and the Budget (OMB) (recently shifted to White House Chief of Staff), and Robert Rubin, head of the new National Economic Council. These conservative senior economic aides fought vigorously with Clinton's more liberal policy advisors for Clinton to emphasize deficit-cutting in his economic program. Second, you should seek to determine how much of a conflict there may be between the politics of the White House and the Fed chairman's fiscal and monetary policy views. While the Fed has enough policy independence to exert adequate credit restraint if it fears a flare-up of inflation, its actions could conceivably be delayed if not moderated in the face of heavy and sustained political criticism. Third, you should determine how long the Fed chairman has been in office and how much respect he or she commands from Washington officials and the general public. When Clinton took the oath as president in January 1993, Greenspan had already been Fed chairman for more than five years. Greenspan's predecessor as Fed chairman, Paul Volcker, was also a highly respected inflation fighter.

The Clinton administration seemed ready to go to almost any

length to show that Greenspan was on board. From the start, to pave the way for his stamp of approval, Greenspan was invited to Little Rock, Arkansas, on December 3, 1992, to meet with President-elect Clinton. From all accounts, the two hit it off remarkably well. To be sure, they were truly an "odd couple"—the serious, urbane, cultured, introverted New Yorker and the smiling, back-slapping, Elvis Presley–admiring, extroverted Southern politician. Greenspan is a loyal Republican with a deep philosophical commitment to free market capitalism and individual initiative, being a disciple in his younger days of Ayn Rand, a fervent proponent of capitalism in its purest form. In contrast, Clinton favors greater reliance on government programs to help people in need and more government regulation. In any case, this "odd couple" at least has in common high intelligence and a fascination with detail.

At the Little Rock meeting, the personal chemistry between these two powerful figures was good, and Greenspan was especially impressed with Clinton's grasp of economic issues. The Little Rock meeting between the Fed Chairman and his new friend was scheduled to last one hour, but it actually continued on for two and a half hours through an unscheduled lunch. Greenspan probably expressed the view that in order for the Clinton administration to bring down long-term interest rates, its economic program had to have credibility in the bond market. Greenspan felt that credible deficit-cutting measures at this critical juncture were absolutely essential and took the opportunity to express this viewpoint.

THE NEC's INFLUENCE ON THE CHIEF EXECUTIVE

The National Economic Council (NEC) was established by President Clinton on the premise that economic policy should be formulated by a team of top advisors and coordinated at a high level among affected agencies. The NEC was modeled after the president's National Security Council, which consists of a team of top foreign policy advisors who formulate and coordinate foreign policy.

President Clinton was right at home in the NEC policy meetings as he intelligently discussed broad policy issues at great length and immersed himself in the details of his economic plan. In NEC meetings, the president savored the opportunity for endless debate over domestic policy options, including how much to cut the deficit. The president's conservative advisors (Bentsen, Panetta, and Rubin) emphasized deficit cutting, while his more liberal advisors, including Robert Reich (labor secretary), Gene Sperling (deputy head of the NEC), political consultants Paul Begala and James Carville, along with George Stephanopoulos (communications director), and the president's wife, Hillary Rodham Clinton, all urged a huge increase in spending on the new domestic programs promised by Clinton in his campaign.

From the beginning, Greenspan also hit it off well with the conservative members of Clinton's economic team, Messrs. Bentsen, Panetta, and Rubin. This team, at a special meeting on January 7, 1993, impressed on President-elect Clinton that his economic program had to be, above all else, "credible" in the bond market. To that end, following some private conversations with Greenspan, Bentsen reportedly scuttled much of the social "investment" program promised in the Clinton campaign platform, despite the effort of the more liberal economic advisors to preserve it.

FED CHAIRMAN'S MOTIVES FOR GOOD RAPPORT

The motives of Fed Chairman Alan Greenspan for cooperation with President Clinton were partly related to prevailing economic circumstances and partly to factors unrelated to the Fed chairman's job. To start with, the president had something the Fed chairman wanted, and the Fed chairman had something the president wanted. Namely, the Fed chairman wanted the president (in cooperation with Congress) to reduce the structural federal budget deficit in order to avoid a possible future financial catastrophe. The Fed chairman was worried that eventually the rate of growth of federal debt-servicing requirements would outpace the rate of growth of our nation's tax base (GDP). In turn, the president wanted the highly respected Fed chairman's support for his economic programs. Clinton knew that Greenspan's support and kind words would give the Clinton administration's economic plan more credibility than it could get from virtually any other source.

Fed Chairman Greenspan also had personal reasons for establishing a good rapport with the new president. They boiled down to the fact that Greenspan wanted to keep this power base in Washington, D.C. The normally shy and self-conscious Greenspan had warmed to the Washington scene during his first term as Fed chairman. It was a heady experience for Greenspan as the second most powerful person in government, far superior to Greenspan's earlier Washington stints as head of President Reagan's Social Security Commission and chairman of President Ford's Council of Economic Advisers. Greenspan relished the high visibility and the challenge of sifting through mountains of data and arriving at the proper diagnosis of the economy's ailments, and then personally directing the appropriate adjustments in Fed policy. Swept up in an increasingly active social life, Greenspan and his companion, Andrea Mitchell, chief White House correspondent for NBC news, seemed to enjoy the limelight.

Perhaps another reason for Greenspan's unusually close relationship with the Executive Branch of government was that he felt it was necessary to hold out the olive branch to the new Democratic president in order to simply assure a good working relationship with the new administration. This was necessary because at the time President Clinton took office the Fed Board of Governors consisted entirely of members who had been appointed by Republican Presidents (Reagan and Bush). In this regard, Greenspan prided himself on his political savvy, based on a wealth of experience and friendships ranging back to the Nixon administration. Indeed, Greenspan had such a high level of confidence in his own political instincts that he felt it was unnecessary in his first term as Fed chairman to appoint a special assistant to help with congressional and White House relations, as his predecessor, Paul Volcker, had done. Most certainly, Greenspan must have found the prospect of getting off on the right foot with the Clinton administration considerably more appealing than a continuation of the harassment suffered under the Bush administration. Furthermore, by encouraging President Clinton to emphasize the deficit-cutting features of his economic program, and then by praising these deficit-cutting intentions, Fed Chairman Greenspan hoped to achieve the desired effect of a decline in stubbornly high long-term interest rates.

Also, there was a good chance that Greenspan's friendship with Clinton might help head off the mounting threat of congressionally sponsored Fed-reform legislation. At least Greenspan could appeal to the president to help block unreasonable congressional Fed-reform efforts. Of course, the threat of Fed-bashing legislation was not new, but now that a Democratic president was in the White House, the threat loomed greater. As far back as the 1950s, designs to weaken the Fed were pushed by populist Congressman Wright Patman (D., Texas); more recently, from 1979 to 1990 no fewer than 200 Fed-reform bills have been submitted to Congress. Undoubtedly, Greenspan (like his predecessors) felt that this political intrusion could jeopardize the Fed's independence and professional integrity. Among the threatening features of Fed-reform legislation proposed by House Banking Committee Chairman Henry Gonzalez (D., Texas), Joint Economic Committee Co-Chairmen Senator Paul Sarbanes (D., Maryland) and Representative Lee Hamilton (D., Indiana) were major changes in the policy role and means of selection of the 12 Reserve Bank presidents, changes in the method of selecting Reserve Bank boards of directors, the immediate publication of Fed policy deliberations, and closer congressional scrutiny of Fed finances.

THE SECRET TAPES

As you seek to understand the Fed as the key to your investment success, it is important to take a closer look at an incident that has led Fed officials to pull back the curtains of secrecy ever so slightly. Fed policy deliberations are in secret and the record of FOMC policy action are not released until 5 to 6 weeks after each scheduled meeting. This is why it was so surprising when, in routine congressional testimony to the House Banking Committee in 1993, Fed Chairman Greenspan let it be known that the monetary authorities kept audio tapes of each FOMC policy meeting for purposes of accurately transcribing comments for the official record of policy actions.

The crusty, stubborn, cantankerous loner who heads the Banking Committee, Representative Henry Gonzalez, was beside himself with glee when news of the existence of the Fed audio tapes, not even known to some Reserve Bank presidents participating in the FOMC meetings, was blurted out by the Fed chairman. Gonzalez had long been urging that the Fed publicly announce any policy shift immediately after the decision was made rather than with the already noted 5- to 6-week delay.

After intense internal Fed deliberations, Chairman Greenspan and his fellow policymakers decided to release transcripts of the FOMC tapes, starting five years earlier in 1988 and working backward. The delay in release of more recent tapes was done in order that current Fed deliberations not be compromised. The primary concern was that individual Fed policymakers would not be completely forthright in expressing their views at FOMC meetings if they knew that every word they uttered was being recorded for public release.

Although Fed officials won't admit it, the embarrassing disclosure of the secret tapes before the House Banking Committee in all likelihood was the last straw in finally motivating the monetary authorities to begin the practice of immediately announcing FOMC policy decisions. Under the blanket of Fed secrecy and the 5- to 6-week delay in announcing Fed actions, there were usually a flurry of press leaks and general financial market confusion about Fed policy intentions.

In contrast, as a budding Fed watcher, you can now learn of Fed actions immediately, a practice that began with the Fed's February 4, 1994, tightening step. To be sure, Fed officials have not yet verified that the new practice of immediately announcing FOMC policy shifts will be permanent. Nevertheless, there has been a subtle but significant shift by the Fed toward more openness in policymaking. The Fed's veil of secrecy has at least been partially lifted.

GREENSPAN'S VIEWS ON DEFICIT-CUTTING

The time-worn adage is that central bankers are paid to worry. Historically, Fed chairmen and their fellow monetary policymakers have mainly worried about *excesses*—notably too much money and credit growth, intensifying pressure on productive resources, mounting wage-cost pressures, and excessive price increases. Fed chairmen have also worried about excessive fiscal stimulus, especially when stepped-up government spending to fight recession usually takes full effect only after the subsequent recovery is well underway, thereby aggravating budding inflationary pressures.

Accordingly, we might have expected that Fed Chairman Greenspan, in his semiannual Humphrey-Hawkins congressional testimony on February 19, 1993, would sound some cautionary notes. At the very least, we could anticipate that the Fed chairman would sound a note of concern about the necessity of avoiding fiscal excesses and the need for the Fed to remain eternally vigilant against inflation. What was not widely known at this time was that Greenspan and Bentsen had already conspired to have a major impact on the Clinton economic program by tilting it away from large social-spending programs toward aggressive deficit-cutting efforts.

It was thus no great surprise that the tone of the Fed chairman's congressional testimony was moderately positive and well disposed toward the Clinton economic plan. Greenspan praised President Clinton's deficit-cutting efforts. The Fed chairman commended President Clinton for placing a serious deficit-cutting plan on the table for active debate. Greenspan endorsed the goal of reducing the structural deficit sharply.

The Fed chairman added that there was no immediate need for the Fed to raise short-term rates because there was still enough slack in the economy to allow it to grow fairly rapidly without the threat of renewed inflationary pressures. Greenspan noted that the Fed and the Clinton administration had the shared goal for the American economy of attaining the largest possible increase in the standard of living for our citizens over time. If the Clinton deficit-cutting plan began to drag down future economic growth, Greenspan said the central bank would "certainly need to take into account" cuts in the federal deficit and their effect on the economy before the Fed decided to adjust short-term interest rates. But Greenspan added that it was not possible for the Fed "to specify in advance what actions might be taken."

Importantly, Greenspan said that a credible plan to cut the deficit would, if enacted, reduce inflationary pressures, and he suggested that this would help drive down long-term interest rates further. Greenspan even went so far as to speculate that the positive economic impact of lower longer-term rates in stimulating business investment and housing activity might help offset the negative economic impact of higher taxes and other deficit-cutting measures proposed by the Clinton administration (which, in fact, turned out to be the case).

The kind of budget restraint measures that Greenspan would

find impressive are things like continued "caps" on discretionary spending and limits on entitlements. (Entitlements are programs to which people are entitled regardless of need such as Social Security and Medicare.) The problem is that the current slowing in the rate of growth of government spending is largely attributable to defense spending cutbacks which will be diminishing in magnitude in coming years. Ultimately, the Fed chairman will be looking for spending restraint measures that result in a persistent decline in the ratio of the deficit to gross domestic product. In these circumstances, the government's claim on domestic savings will recede, exerting downward pressure on long-term interest rates and making more funds available on attractive borrowing terms to finance business spending on new plant and equipment.

RISKS IN THE CHAIRMAN-PRESIDENT RELATIONSHIP

Chairman Greenspan's unexpectedly cordial relationship with President Clinton carries some risks. The risks include global investors' perception that the Fed chairman is willing to sacrifice needed credit-tightening moves for purposes of curtailing inflation on the altar of White House promises of future fiscal restraint. Also, there is the possible market perception that the president could play on his close working relationship with Greenspan to urge the Fed chairman to postpone any credit-tightening moves until after elections. In addition, the White House might take advantage of its close and friendly Fed ties to urge that the Fed forgo necessary credit-tightening steps at times when the White House may be trying to talk the U.S. dollar lower to reduce the U.S. trade deficit. (A lower dollar makes U.S. exports less expensive and imports more expensive.)

This slightest hint that the Fed may be contemplating postponing appropriate credit-tightening moves to head off renewed inflationary pressures would likely be promptly reflected in a disorderly plunge in the dollar, rising commodity prices, and an unwelcomed spike in long-term interest rates. Contributing to this upward pressure on long-term interest rates would be sales of U.S. bonds by foreign investors facing losses from the declining dollar.

ANATOMY OF A FED POLICY SHIFT

You can make sense out of Fed policy shifts, and thus make successful portfolio adjustments that increase your return and reduce your risk, if you follow closely the anatomy of a Fed policy shift. This is a good way to learn to watch what the Fed watches. And if you religiously follow this cardinal rule of Fed watching, you may even surprise yourself by being able to anticipate Fed policy shifts from time to time.

By analyzing a significant Fed policy shift that had a major impact on the bond and stock markets, you can gain insight into what motivates Fed policymakers to initiate a series of tightening steps. The Fed policy shift focused on is the February 4, 1994 tightening action, the first in five years.

January 21, 1994   On this day there was an unannounced meeting reportedly arranged by NEC head Rubin between Fed Chairman Greenspan, President Clinton, and his other top economic advisors. This meeting came on the heels of a whopping 7.5% increase in real GDP in the fourth quarter of 1993. (In two subsequent revisions, this figure was first revised to a 7% increase and then to a 6.3% gain.) White House advisors were suddenly worried that the surprisingly good economic performance might peak in 1994, or at the latest in 1995, rather than continuing through the critical 1996 presidential election year. The Fed chairman and the president apparently agreed at this meeting that a preemptive Fed strike against future inflationary pressures might not be a bad idea. Specifically, it was presumably decided that the Fed could act promptly to raise short-term rates so as to keep inflationary expectations in check and hopefully limit any rise in long-term interest rates, thereby prolonging the recovery.

January 31, 1994   If you were seeking to anticipate the Fed's impending tightening move, you should have read closely the public testimony by Fed Chairman Greenspan before the Joint Economic Committee on this day. In no uncertain terms, the Fed chairman warned that the Fed had decided to act sooner rather than later to move away from a friendly credit policy that had made funds abundantly available at low interest rates to consumers and business borrowers. In turn, these borrowers were able to refinance their heavy debt burdens from the 1980s at lower interest rates, thus greatly relieving their heavy debt servicing burdens. Mortgage borrowers engaged in four major waves of mortgage refinancing in late 1991, mid-1992, early 1993, and mid-1993. In addition, many businesses were able to not only refinance their debt at lower interest rates, but also to pay off debt with funds raised in the rallying equity market. In this testimony, Greenspan noted that "the foundations of economic expansion are looking increasingly well-entrenched." You might say to yourself that this is a rather bland way of putting people on notice that a Fed credit-tightening move is coming. But remember, when the Fed chairman sees the positive side on the economic picture, he is probably getting ready to crash the party. (Greenspan's predecessor, Paul Volcker, once related that a friend of his once walked up to him and said, "You central bankers are all alike; you are forever afraid that somewhere, someone is happy.") More ominously, Greenspan observed "short-term interest rates are currently abnormally low in real terms," adding that eventually "we will need to move them to a more neutral stance." These comments suggested that once the Fed started tightening credit, it would likely follow its first step with several more as it moved the Fed's policy stance from friendly (accommodative) to "neutral." Presumably an accommodative stance was aimed at improving the financial foundation of the economy so as to give a boost to the pace of recovery. Alternatively a "neutral" Fed policy stance implied that the Fed was seeking to neither stimulate nor depress economic activity. (As matters turned out, the Fed took four tightening steps in the move from an accommodative policy stance to a neutral policy stance; specifically these tightening steps occurred in February, March, April, and May of 1994.)

February 3–4, 1994   At the two-day FOMC policy meeting, Fed officials decided on the now infamous February 4, 1994, tightening move that hammered down the value of your bond and stock mutual funds. Among the items you should watch for in the record of each FOMC policy meeting is how surprised the Fed policymakers were concerning the strength of the recovery. And, more important, you should note the extent to which the monetary authorities were worried about early signs of a future acceleration in inflationary pressures, such as growing pressure on productivity capacity, rising commodity prices, increasing delivery lead times associated voluntary business inventory building, and rising credit growth. You should also watch for general Fed comments to the effect that the economy is expected to continue to grow at a pace above the economy's long-run potential. There is a virtually guaranteed prescription for additional future Fed-tightening steps when higher than potential growth rates persist at an advanced stage of recovery.

At the February 3–4, 1994, FOMC meeting, Fed policymakers commented that "the economy had entered the new year with appreciable forward momentum and that the expansion was likely to be sustained over the year ahead at a pace somewhat above the economy's long-run potential." The monetary authorities went on to warn that "[i]n the context of low and decreasing slack in the economy, little further progress would be made toward price stability in 1994, and there was a distinct risk of higher inflation at some point if monetary policy were not adjusted." Commenting on other conditions possibly leading to increased price pressures, Fed officials warned that "lean inventory levels in the context of diminishing slack in labor and product markets raised concerns about the potential for increasing capacity pressures should strong demands persist that would tend to deplete existing inventories and lead to efforts not only to rebuild but to increase them." Fed officials also noted "reports of shortages of skilled workers in some parts of the country" and of "rising prices for products being purchased by business firms for use in the production process and in turn of successful efforts by businesses to raise their own prices in order to pass on higher costs or to improve their profit margins." Fed policymakers concluded that "a relatively small [tightening] move would readily accomplish the purpose of signalling the [FOMC's] anti-inflation resolve and together with expected further action should help to temper or avert an increase in inflation expectations and speculative developments in financial markets."

A SHOCKING FINANCIAL MARKET RESPONSE

The magnitude of the bond yields' surge in response to the Fed's modest tightening steps surprised even seasoned investors. Normally, a moderate increase in long-term rates is expected in response to a Fed move to tighten credit and push short-term rates higher. It would not have shocked most market participants if long-term rates rise, say, one-half percentage point for every Fed-induced increase of one percentage point in short-term rates. But what was shocking in the case of the Fed's first three tightening steps in early 1994 was that a Fed-induced increase of three quarters of one percentage point in short-term rates triggered a whopping increase of roughly one and a half percentage points in long-term rates.

When the bond market's response seems disproportionate to Fed policy shifts, that is the Fed watcher's cue to look for other financial shifts that may have reinforced or even exacerbated the Fed's actions. In early 1994, for instance, there was a totally unexpected collapse in the U.S. dollar in terms of the Japanese yen following the February 11 breakdown in trade talks between the United States and Japan and the mushrooming threat of a trade war. After the collapse of the trade talks, it was feared that the Clinton administration wanted the dollar to fall in terms of the yen in order to reduce the Japanese trade surplus. With the prospect for a further weakening in the dollar, global investors dumped large amounts of dollar-denominated securities.

The global interdependence of financial markets was also vividly demonstrated in the wake of the Fed's February 4, 1994, credit-tightening action. The resulting weakness in the U.S. bond market spread quickly to fixed-income markets in Europe and Asia. Among the heavy sellers of fixed-income securities and equities around the world were highly leveraged hedge funds that had bet heavily that the U.S. bond market rally would be repeated in other major countries at earlier stages of recovery, and thus had come into 1994 heavily invested in foreign bonds. Large hedge funds, which may hold leveraged speculative positions far in excess of their capital, suffered huge losses in this financial market frenzy. The capital of these leveraged hedge funds, which are private investment partnerships for wealthy individuals and institutions, has been estimated at $80 billion or more. Since these hedge funds typically leverage their capital 5 to 10 times, this means that these hedge funds can have command of possibly as much as $400 billion to $800 billion in funds for global speculative investments.

Smaller purses can also impact the financial markets. Individual investors rushed to redeem their bond mutual funds in the wake of the Fed's February 4, 1994, tightening move. In turn, the beleaguered bond mutual funds, which had invested heavily in illiquid, high-risk, long-term bonds and derivatives in order to earn a higher return that would attract more investors, were forced to sell off portions of their portfolios thus exerting additional upward pressure on interest rates. Also exerting upward pressure on interest rates were technical problems in the $1.6 trillion mortgage-backed securities market, in the wake of the Fed-induced spike in short-term interest rates (see Chapter 10).

We always have to also look for a political dimension to volatility in the financial markets. In early 1994, the growing concerns that the Whitewater scandal was affecting the Clinton administration's credibility exerted upward pressure on bond yields. In addition, there were fears that growing tensions between the United States and North Korea would add to defense costs and put the Clinton administration's deficit-cutting efforts in jeopardy, thereby leading to greater competition for limited domestic savings between the government, private business, and individual borrowers.

Section Three

PROFITING FROM THE OPENING
OF THE FINANCIAL MARKETS

Y ou have to be impressed with the wondrous array of investment options that the modern financial markets offer. But to be successful in this contemporary world of endless investment opportunities, you must work harder than in the past. To start with, you need to give some thought to your main investment goal and how you plan to achieve it. At the heart of this process is the need to strike a balance between risk and return with which you are comfortable. In this connection, the split you choose between stocks and bonds in your portfolio bears directly on your portfolio's risk-return characteristics.

Next, you should choose an investment approach. Your basic choices are income, value, growth, and maximum short-term capital appreciation. At one extreme, if you are a very conservative investor you might favor a portfolio that generates a steady, predictable and dependable flow of income. At the other extreme, you may be a highly aggressive investor with a great tolerance for risk aiming at maximum short-term capital appreciation.

In order to try to achieve portfolio diversification as protection against unforeseen shocks that might affect some of your investments but not others, you might include in your portfolio U.S. stocks and bonds, foreign stocks and bonds, and high-yield or illiquid debt. Included in this high-yield debt category might be mortgage pass throughs and their derivatives such as collateralized mortgage obligations (CMOs). Derivatives are financial instruments whose value is linked to some underlying asset. You must remember that mortgage derivatives such as CMOs can at times become highly illiquid and volatile and thus should make up only a relatively modest portion of your investment portfolio.

An important feature of your new investment horizon is the eclipse of commercial banks as sources of liquidity. Your investment relationship with banks may be changing for good. Faced with government overregulation, banks are changing the way they do business with you and your investor friends. These days banks don't offer you as competitive a rate on CDs as they did in the past. Instead, banks have become accustomed to a wide spread between the low rates they pay for CD money and the higher interest rates they earn on loans and investments. In a fundamental way, banks are turning increasingly to off-balance-sheet activities like interest rate and currency swap activities. In addition, an increasing number of banks find it beneficial to securitize their loans. Specifically, after they earn a fee for originating loans, banks will sell them off their balance sheets into the capital markets to serve as a basis for mortgage-backed or asset-backed securities. In turn, either directly or through mutual funds, you and fellow individual investors can invest in this wide variety of newly securitized instruments. In this way, you find the capital markets increasingly dominating banks as the source of your investment options.

On the international front as well, global investing is not just for the millionaire stock speculators, it's for everyone seeking to diversify their portfolio. Although the advice of top investment advisors differs in terms of the percentages (from 10% to 40%), they all agree that some portion of your assets should reside in global investments.

Even so, with these new global investment opportunities come sobering risks and responsibilities. You have to consider and monitor the political risk, foreign currency fluctuations, and special economic circumstances that are associated with these investments. Moreover, on a note of caution, you should be aware that in periods of great financial market volatility, U.S. and foreign stocks and bonds tend to move together, especially to the downside.

Don't underestimate potential foreign exchange volatility and how this might eat into your earnings on foreign bonds and stocks. Of course, U.S. investors must convert their dollars into the appropriate currency before making an investment in foreign stocks or bonds. Likewise, when you want to sell foreign stocks or bonds you must convert the local currency received in the sale back into dollars. You can hedge these currency transactions with futures or options designed to lock in a certain exchange rate, but this costs money and thus diminishes your return on foreign investments. There are other important considerations that we'll examine in the chapters that follow.

6

Identifying Your Best Investment
Options Among Many

The more quickly you master the many investment options available to you, the more quickly you can achieve your dream of financial independence. The first step is to think about your primary investment objective. Only you can know what is most important to you in terms of your personal finances. Perhaps your goal is a short-term one of buying your first home or funding a European vacation in the near future. Or maybe it's a longer-term one of funding your child's education or retiring before age 60. Or maybe you have already retired and you want to find a low-risk way to increase your principal by more than 10% each year. Whatever the case, once you have settled upon your primary investment goal, write it down and begin to map out the steps that will lead you to it.

SELECTING AN INVESTMENT APPROACH

Once you have selected your primary objective, the next step is to choose an approach to reach that end. There are four major investment approaches: income, value, growth, and short-term capital appreciation. Here's a quick overview of each approach:

Income An income-oriented investment approach appeals to investors who want an adequate, dependable, and predictable stream of income. Investors following this approach typically have a low tolerance for risk. Income investors may be dependent on inter-

est income and stock dividends generated by their investment portfolio to support their day-to-day living needs. A portfolio designed
to produce a steady income flow usually favors intermediate-term
(5- to 10-year) Treasury securities and high-dividend stocks.

Value   Investors following a value approach are seeking
stocks that look cheap compared with others. They feel they can
stomach a small to moderate amount of risk and are looking for
stocks that are a good buy based on the price of the stocks compared with earnings, cash, assets, or some other measure of intrin-
sic value. A good example of a value-oriented investment approach
in the early 1990s was to buy financial stocks which had been bat-
tered down to bargain levels by the widely publicized savings and
loan crisis of the late 1980s.

Growth   If you have a moderately good appetite for risk, you
might favor stocks with rapidly rising sales and earnings. Growth
stocks usually cost more than other stocks, but investors say it's
worth paying a premium for them because eventually the growth
stock's price will reflect rising profits. Growth-oriented portfolios
tend to favor such areas as technology, food, communications, en-
tertainment, and medicine. The two major types of growth stocks
are those of *quality* growth stocks, or those of successful, glam-
orous companies that have already won market approval, such as a
company like Coca-Cola, or *emerging* growth stocks like those of
smaller but promising beverage companies.

Short-Term Capital Appreciation   Investors seeking maximum short-term capital appreciation have the greatest tolerance for
risk. They will seek out the stock of any company, large or small,
that has the potential for rapid short-term appreciation. The pur-
suit of maximum short-term capital appreciation typically involves
rapid equity portfolio turnover, leveraging, and extensive trading in
derivatives such as stock index futures, options, or options on futures.

Most important, you should select the investment approach
that best fits your needs. The idea is to give considerable attention
to your financial circumstances, your tolerance for risk and the

length of your investment horizon in selecting an investment approach. For example, if you are a retiree who has little stomach for risk, and a relatively short-term investment horizon, you unquestionably should choose the income-centered investment approach. Alternatively, if you are a successful middle-aged executive with a sizable savings nest egg who is seeking a 10% or better annual return on your investment portfolio as you prepare for retirement, you might choose a growth-centered investment approach, perhaps consisting of half *quality* growth stocks and half *emerging* growth stocks.

If you choose either the value or the growth approach to investing, you will probably be happiest with a balanced portfolio consisting of half to two-thirds stocks and half to one-third bonds. To offset the greater risk in the stock portion of your portfolio, you need to balance your portfolio with bond holdings that operate as a kind of security blanket, giving you peace of mind. Of course, bonds can also suffer capital losses if interest rates rise. But the central message of this book is that you can minimize the threat of bond losses by making crucial adjustments in your fixed-income holdings tied to certain Federal Reserve policy shifts.

UNDERSTANDING YOUR INVESTMENT OPTIONS

Suddenly, the sky is the limit in your choice of investments. Your next step is to understand the options available to you such as U.S. bonds and stocks, foreign bonds and stocks, high-yield debt, and derivatives. (Derivatives are financial instruments whose value is based on, or derived from, assets such as stocks, bonds, commodities, or foreign exchanges.)

In terms of a degree of credit risk, your safest investments are *Treasury* bills, notes, and bonds that are backed by the full faith and credit of the U.S. government. You don't have to stay awake nights worrying about whether the U.S. government will make its interest and principal payments to holders of its obligations. *Agency* bonds are issued by government agencies or government-sponsored enterprises and carry an implicit government promise to pay interest and principal owed you and your fellow investors. Carrying somewhat greater credit risk are *corporate* bonds. You should make use of the corporate bond credit ratings of the two major credit rating services, Moody's Investors Service, Inc., and Standard & Poor's Corp., in picking investment-grade corporate bonds. Moody's safest investment grade ratings are Aaa, Aa, and A, and the comparable S & P top three credit ratings are AAA, AA, and A. *High-yield* (junk) corporate bonds carry lower, more speculative, ratings or, in some cases, no rating at all. Needless to say, these junk bonds carry a much greater credit risk. Just the same, their high yield can make them an attractive investment option. Next in order of credit risk are large blue-chip growth *stocks* usually represented by the S & P 500 stock index, followed by small-company stocks perhaps best represented by the Russell 2000 stock index.

As you ponder these investment options, you might be interested in comparing their total returns over an extended time period. During the past *century*, stocks have earned an annual average total return of about 10%; bonds, 6 to 7%; and liquid, short-term investments, 3%. Remember, when you buy a company's stock you become an owner of a piece of that company and share in its profits by receiving dividends. Alternatively, when you buy a company's (or the government's) bonds, you are simply lending money to that company (or government) and will, in return, receive fixed interest payments and eventual repayment of principal. Underscoring that stocks carry a greater credit risk than bonds is the fact that when a company fails and its assets are liquidated, bond holders are paid off before stockholders.

INVESTING THAT LUMP SUM

For those of you who may have been caught in the web of 1990s corporate layoffs, and who may be leaving your company with a good-sized severance payment and 401(k) settlement, you are facing a big and important investment decision that you must make quickly (or suffer sizable tax consequences). Presently, more than 40 million Americans have 401(k) plans. Just remember not to panic, and don't take investment shortcuts. The last thing you should do in this situation is to hire a financial planner to take charge of investing this large sum without first checking that person's background. Many investors are biased in favor of fee-only financial planners who do not receive commission on the products you ultimately select and who, thereby, have no hidden agenda of selling you an investment because of the commission it will win them. Even after hiring an investment advisor who may come well recommended, you must decide upon your primary investment goal and continuously monitor this person's approach and results toward reaching that goal. Rather than turn to an investment advisor, you might choose to invest your lump sum in a single growth-oriented equity mutual fund with a good 5-year performance record—depending, of course, upon the make up of your existing portfolio.

Alternatively, you might invest your lump-sum payment in several specialized mutual funds, which have uncorrelated returns. This multifund investing approach might include a short-term money market fund, an intermediate bond fund, a capital appreciation equity fund, and an emerging growth equity fund. Remember, it is extremely important that you continuously monitor this multifund portfolio. To remain alert to problems, you should check the performance of each of your mutual funds at least monthly.

INVESTING YOUR PENSION

Two additional pieces of advice should be heeded by those of you who are lucky enough to keep your job during the 1990s corporate restructuring binge. (1) Contribute the maximum allowable amount to your 401(k) and take advantage of the associated tax break. Make sure, though, that you don't own too much of your employer's stock in your profit-sharing or 401(k) retirement plans. If you hold too much corporate stock, it could mean "double trouble" for you if your company runs into hard times and you lose your job while the value of your company stock plunges. (2) Avoid pulling your money out of your 401(k) retirement plan and individual retirement accounts before you reach the age of $59\frac{1}{2}$. You will end up paying 40% in federal, state, and local taxes—plus a 10% penalty for taking the money out early. To avoid losing half your

retirement nest egg in this manner, you should instead take a loan
from your retirement plan, if you need the money to tide you over,
and then pay yourself back over several years.

DIVERSIFYING YOUR PORTFOLIO

A major theme of this book is that you need to strike a balance between risk and return in your portfolio. In this connection, your
key decision will be the split between stocks and bonds in your
portfolio. Within these basic financial asset categories your adjustments can, in turn, be determined by your investment approach
and by watching for U.S. economic turning points and Fed responses.

　　Once you have decided on an investment approach, you next
should seek to achieve portfolio diversification. The basic idea of
diversification is to invest in assets that do not move closely together over time. One way to achieve portfolio diversification
might be through a five-item investment strategy, consisting of U.S.
stocks, investment-grade U.S. bonds, foreign stocks, foreign bonds,
and high-yield debt and derivatives. Within your U.S. equity portfolio you might, in turn, split your holdings according to industry
size (small cap, mid-cap, and large cap), and according to investment approach (value, growth, etc.). Moreover, within your foreign
stock holdings you can split your holding between emerging and
developed markets. Your high-yield debt might consist of corporate
junk bonds, mortgage-backed securities, or even their collateralized
mortgage obligation derivatives. You can achieve this five-item investment strategy by investing directly, or through mutual funds, or
preferably some combination of each.

IDENTIFYING MUTUAL FUND INVESTMENT OPTIONS

A typical mutual fund family offers investment diversification in
such areas as equity, fixed-income, balanced (equity and fixed-income), international, money market, and municipals. Within a mutual fund family, each investment sector can operate as a separate
diversified entity. The investment objective of each area is typically

described in the mutual fund's prospectus. Mutual fund families might include separate investment categories like domestic diversified equities, individual sector equities, domestic taxable fixed-income, tax-exempt (municipal) fixed income, balanced, and money market.

It is important to note that the fixed-income, balanced, international, and municipal portfolios in a typical mutual fund family may invest to varying degrees in high-yield, below-investment-grade securities. These mutual funds also invest in mortgage-backed securities or their derivatives such as CMOs. You should inquire from your mutual fund family sponsor precisely what proportion of its investments are accounted for by such illiquid high-risk securities. Any proportion above 10% is extremely dangerous.

If you have a limited amount of time to dedicate to investing or if you are not wholly confident in your investment selection abilities, you will most likely find mutual funds the most attractive and convenient investment approach. Mutual funds can offer a large measure of portfolio diversification, consistent with your investment objective. However, this should not preclude the possibility of a mixed investment approach in which you invest indirectly through domestic and international equity mutual funds and international fixed-income mutual funds, while at the same time investing directly in a domestic fixed-income portfolio, conceivably consisting mostly or entirely of Treasury securities. Again, your choice will flow from the amount of time you donate to investing and the level of risk you're willing to assume.

SOME SPECIAL INVESTMENT VEHICLES

Before you finalize your selection of investment vehicles, here are four special opportunities for your consideration:

Treasury Direct   If you are a 1990s-type of investor who hates to pay for something that you can get free, you need to know that there is a program called Treasury Direct which allows you to buy new Treasury bills, notes, and bonds directly from the Treasury with no sales or management fees. The process involves filling out an application, which you can obtain from the nearest office of your district Federal Reserve Bank (your local banker will have the appropriate address and telephone number). For 3- and 6-month Treasury bills which are auctioned weekly on Monday (and issued the following Thursday), you must deliver, along with the application, a certified check or cashier's check for the amount you intend to buy. New Treasury bills in denominations of 3 and 6 months are sold in minimum face value amounts of $10,000. Additional auctions of 12-month bills are sold, also in $10,000 face amounts, and are held every fourth week, usually on a Thursday. One useful feature of the Treasury Direct system is that you can request a reinvestment of your maturing 3-, 6-, and 12-month bills for a period of up to 104 weeks.

Alternatively, you can bid directly from the Treasury for new notes due in two or three years, which come in minimums of $5,000, and new notes or bonds with maturities of more than three years, which have minimum face value amounts of $1,000. Additional amounts beyond the face value can be purchased in increments of $1,000. The auction schedules of 2- and 5-year notes are at the end of each month, while 3- and 10-year notes are auctioned quarterly in February, May, August, and November. The Treasury auctions its longest-term 30-year bonds semiannually in February and August.

American Depository Receipts   If you decide to invest directly in foreign equities rather than indirectly through mutual funds, you should consider American depository receipts (ADRs). These ADRs are certificates that represent the ownerships of foreign stocks that are in fact held abroad, usually by big U.S. banks with foreign operations. The ADR allows you as an individual investor to receive all the dividends and capital appreciation that the actual stock abroad enjoys, and, thus, for all practical purposes, owning ADRs is just like owning the stock. The nice thing about ADRs is that they can be purchased in dollars, and their dividends are paid in dollars (adjusted, of course, for currency fluctuations and administrative fees). Striking a more cautious note, you should be aware that ADRs are available only for the biggest and best known foreign companies. Limiting your foreign equity investments to ADRs thus precludes you from shares of small, rapidly growing foreign companies that often produce the most spectacular gains on foreign stock exchanges. For this reason, you should usually favor global mutual funds with a good longer-term track record as the means of investing in foreign equities.

Variable Annuities   One way you can both own mutual funds and enjoy a tax benefit as well is to purchase variable annuities. Just like the old individual retirement accounts (IRAs) for which many of us no longer qualify, you can invest in a variable annuity by putting up a lump sum of money that is invested in your choice of mutual funds run by the offering institution, which might be an insurance company, brokerage firm, or bank. Like the old IRAs, your dividends and capital gains are not taxed until you withdraw these funds. As an additional bonus, the contracts for variable annuities provide that if you die, your heirs will receive at least the amount you invested in the variable annuity, regardless of the performance of the investments you selected.

The main disadvantages of variable annuities are that the mutual funds offered by the firms selling variable annuities typically underperform other funds. In addition, the fees charged on variable annuities are quite high. Thus, if you happen to be a conservative investor who chooses to invest primarily in short-term, low-risk funds, you may end up paying more in fees on your variable annuity than you make in income. A better course of action is to study closely the 5-year performance record of the funds offered by firms selling variable annuities. The idea is to pick the highest performer with the lowest fee.

Fidelty Funds Network   If you are looking for a break on the transactions fees on the sale of mutual funds, try Fidelity Funds Network. Fidelity offers 86 of its 202 funds without a transactions fee. In total, Fidelity's no-transactions-fee program offers 327 funds from 32 mutual fund families including Fidelity. The Fidelity Funds Network offers a 24-hour 800 number (800 544–9697). Among the features of this plan are trading via computer and a user-friendly performance directory for mutual funds plus an Investment Planner that explains how to invest across asset classes. Under this no-fee program, if you want to move part of your investment portfolio into cash, you would be limited to using Fidelity's money market funds. It should be noted that while Charles Schwab's One Source offers much the same type of no-fee programs, several of the largest and most respected mutual fund families such as Scudder,

Vanguard, and T. Rowe Price don't yet offer the service. The no-fee programs allow easy shifts in asset allocation between stocks, bonds, and money market investments.

TIMING AND SELECTING YOUR INVESTMENTS

If you subscribe to the five-item investment strategy that includes both U.S. and foreign stock and bond investments, along with high-yield bonds and derivatives, you should be aware that during periods of extreme financial market volatility *all* domestic and foreign equity and bond markets tend to move together. This remarkable global capital market linkage during periods of extreme volatility was most recently in evidence on the heels of the Fed's February 4, 1994, tightening move. This tendency of global bond and equity markets to move together during periods of extreme volatility reflects increasing global integration, deregulation, financial innovation, and advanced information technology and communications. The unwinding of massive global leveraged speculation in both stocks and bonds in all major markets was the specific reason for this phenomenon in early 1994.

In this connection, it is important to point out that international investment diversification is still in its adolescence. The costs of gathering, processing, and transmitting information, as well as executing financial transactions, will almost certainly decline further with greater advances in technology. With banks being increasingly stifled by excessive regulation, a growing pool of savings and leverage is in the hands of new nonbank global money managers such as hedge funds, mutual funds, pension funds, insurance companies, and finance companies. This has resulted in the creation of an enormous global pool of mobile, and relatively liquid, capital. This mobile capital pool shifts rapidly and powerfully across national borders, telescoping into a few days or weeks major foreign exchange adjustments or other changes in bond or stock market valuations that might have taken many months or years in the past.

If your investment goal is, say, to earn 10% or more on your portfolio and you can tolerate only moderate risk over an investment time horizon of perhaps up to 25 years, you can begin with half to two-thirds of your portfolio in stocks and with half to one-third in long-term bonds. Your major portfolio shifts should be conditioned by the interaction between the economy and Fed policy shifts. For example, if the Fed tightens credit three times in a row in the advanced stage of recovery in anticipation of the threat of accelerating inflationary pressures, you should sell *all* your long-term bonds and invest half the proceeds in safe and liquid 3-month Treasury bills and half in 5-year Treasury notes. The yield on 5-year notes can represent as much as 85% or more of the yield on 30-year Treasury bonds with only 50% of the volatility.

Conversely, if the Fed eases credit three or more times against the background of a weakening economy and declining inflationary pressures, you should sell your 3-month bills and 5-year notes and invest all the proceeds in 30-year Treasury bonds.

Of course, you might consider some variations on this basic investment strategy. For example, if inflation expectations are increasing you should shift a portion of your stock holdings into real estate or at least into stocks related to real assets such as natural resources. In addition, it is extremely important to seek diversification within your stock and bond holdings.

PUTTING IT ALL TOGETHER

As an individual investor, your best investment options are to build a diversified portfolio consisting of U.S. equities and fixed-income securities, foreign equities and fixed-income securities, and depending on your tolerance of risk, high-yield debt. Once you have determined your investment objective, the most efficient and least time-intensive approach is to invest indirectly through mutual funds for all these portfolio items, except your U.S. Treasury securities. For this item, you should use the Treasury Direct approach. When the economy is in the advanced stages of recovery and the Fed has tightened credit availability three or more times, you should use Treasury Direct to buy 3-month Treasury bills and 5-year Treasury notes. Conversely, when the economy slips toward recession and the Fed responds by easing the availability of credit three or more times, you should use Treasury Direct to buy 30-year Treasury bonds.

For purposes of making these Fed portfolio adjustments, you should simply split your portfolio into basic categories of stocks, bonds, and cash. For example, let's say you start with a $250,000 investment portfolio consisting of $150,000 in stocks, $100,000 in bonds, and no cash. Following three consecutive Fed-tightening steps, you should sell all your bonds and buy $50,000 liquid 3-month bills and $50,000 5-year Treasury notes. The portfolio now consists of $150,000 stocks, no bonds, $50,000 intermediate notes, and $50,000 in liquid bills. Further, if inflationary pressures are threatening to rise for a considerable period of time, you should sell 25% of your equity holdings and invest the proceeds in real estate or natural resource funds. Thus, during periods in which the Fed is tightening credit in order to fight rising inflationary pressures, your portfolio would consist of $112,500 in stocks, $50,000 in 5-year Treasury notes, $50,000 in 3-month Treasury bills (cash), and $37,500 in real assets such as real estate or natural resource funds.

INVESTING MYTHS

1. *Younger persons should invest more aggressively than older ones.* In fact, age is not the key factor influencing how aggressively you invest. Instead, the aggressiveness of your investment approach, at any age, depends on what your objective is, how much risk you can tolerate, and the time horizon for the achievement of your objective.

2. *Portfolio diversification is guaranteed by investing in U.S. and foreign stock and bonds.* This is not always the case. For example, when there is great volatility in the global financial markets in response to a shock like the Fed's credit-tightening move on February 4, 1994, the U.S. and foreign stock and bond markets will all decline together.

3. *Your short-term government securities mutual fund is safe and insured by the government just like your former holdings of bank CDs.* In reality your short-term government securities mutual fund is not insured by the government. Moreover, if your short-term government securities mutual fund has relied excessively on derivatives to boost earnings, it may suffer a sharp contraction. For example, those money market funds that relied excessively on derivatives to boost earnings when short-term interest rates were unusually low in 1993 have subsequently suffered huge losses in the wake of the Fed-induced increase in short-term interest rates in 1994.

4. *You should not concern yourself with any conflicts of interest involving the personal investments of your mutual fund managers.* You should monitor the investments of your fund manager in initial public offerings (IPOs), or in the businesses of the manager's friends and family. Extreme conflicts of interest can depress your fund's earnings performance leading to heavy redemptions. Check both your fund manager's conflicts of interest and his or her earnings record over the past 5 years or longer.

5. *There is no way to protect yourself from a down market in stocks and bonds.* Quite the contrary, you should act according to the principal that a good offense is the best defense. First, during periods when inflationary pressures are mounting, the Fed is tightening credit, and interest rates are climbing, you should sell all your long-term bonds and invest half the proceeds in safer shorter-term investments. Second, you should try to diversify into foreign bond and stock mutual funds, especially in countries that are lagging behind the United States in the timing of their recoveries. Finally, if inflation expectations are on the rise, you should lighten up on financial assets in favor of real assets like real estate or natural resource funds.

7

The Eclipse of Bank CDs

You have just participated in the most revolutionary decade in U.S. financial markets since the Great Depression. The 1980s have seen the collapse of the thrift industry; an unprecedented decline in commercial banks' market share; and a major increase in the market share of mutual funds, pension funds, hedge funds, and other new institutional investment powerhouses. The past decade has also seen trading in foreign securities soar to new heights, along with explosive growth in derivatives markets, both on and off registered exchanges. And these forces have extended into the early 1990s.

During this same period, you have also experienced the eclipse of the bank CD. Your attention has shifted away from plain vanilla bank CDs in favor of the dazzling array of investment opinions offered by rapidly growing mutual funds. Certainly, mutual funds are not new. They first vaulted into popularity in the 1960s, and then fell out of favor in the 1970s. Nevertheless, mutual funds now appear to be here to stay as the primary investment medium of individual investors, and bank CDs are correspondingly on the decline.

The Fed's aggressive credit-easing actions in the early 1990s helped reduce the yield on CDs to record low levels, acting as possibly the final nail in the coffin for these instruments. But the eclipse of the bank CD actually goes much deeper into the issues of a fundamental change in bank behavior, at a time of spectacular financial innovation and global financial integration.

Banks have, for example, come increasingly around to view that in this new environment they should be maximizing profits and not size. Thus they are quick to lower CD rates when the Fed is easing and slow to raise CD rates when the Fed is tightening.

The contrast with conditions only a little more than a decade ago is striking. In the earlier era, it was easy for you to be a passive saver. You could simply place your extra money in a bank CD and forget about it. After all, your bank CD was perfectly safe (being insured up to $100,000 by the government), with unrestricted access, and redeemable at par at maturity. Moreover, in the late 1970s and early 1980s you could get spectacular, double-digit interest rates on these safe and liquid bank CDs. At that time, you might have asked yourself why you should go to the trouble of finding alternative investment options.

ROLE OF THE BANKING SYSTEM

The U.S. banking system has traditionally been at the center of a process referred to as the intermediation process. Through this so-called intermediation process, huge amounts of savings are pooled as deposits and channeled into loans and investments in support of economic growth. Fundamentally, banks provide an intermediation function that results in depositors receiving rates that are lower than yields on loans and investments, in return for increased safety, liquidity, and payments services. The intermediation process, in turn, is predicated on the ability of banks to develop specialized information on the creditworthiness of borrowers and to use this information in ways that take advantage of portfolio diversification.

Historically, banks have been the centerpiece of the financial system. This brings more funds into circulation by attracting demand deposits and time deposits. Given that central function as an important source of liquidity, the stability of the banking system is considered essential for economic well-being. To guarantee stability, the federal government insures bank deposits and rigorously regulates banks to maintain their solvency.

The banking system is the central conduit for monetary policy. Every additional dollar of new reserves the Fed supplies has the potential to add several dollars to the banking system's loans and investments (credit) and deposits (money). Thus, Fed-easing efforts aimed at increasing the availability of credit and lowering its cost (interest rates) operate to stimulate economic activity. Conversely,

Fed-tightening efforts aimed at reducing the availability of credit and increasing its cost operate to restrain economic activity.

During the period from 1960 to 1975, banks and other types of depository institutions such as savings banks and savings and loan associations flourished, expanding their share of total domestic nonfinancial debt to about 55% from just over 40% (see Figure 7.1). During this 15-year period, the introduction of large negotiable CDs and Eurodollar deposits held by corporations and other large institutions helped to fuel bank growth.

At their zenith, banks and other depository institutions accounted for about two-thirds of all mortgage financing activity. At the same time, banks were the credit lifeline for countless small and medium-sized businesses. Alternative capital market sources of credit were at this time poorly developed, and generally available only to the large or "name" corporations that raised money through debt and equity offerings.

The process of shifting business credit from bank to nonbank sources actually began in the 1960s with the development of the commercial paper market. Commercial paper is unsecured short-

Figure 7.1   **Depository Institutions' Share of Total Nonfinancial Debt, 1960–1993**

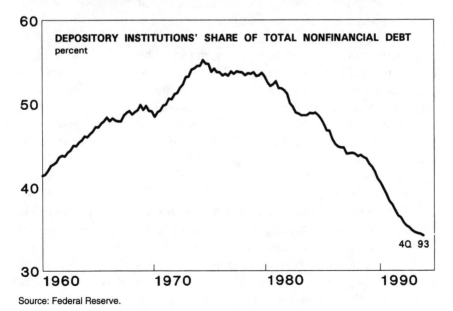

Source: Federal Reserve.

term corporate debt that may be sold to mutual funds, insurance companies, pension funds, or other investors. In the 1980s came high-yield (junk) corporate bonds, through which the low-rated, or non-rated, business borrowers that in the past had to rely solely on banks as their source of funds, could now raise money from alternative capital market sources. These junk bonds fell on hard times in 1990–91, but then bounced back in 1992–93 in large part because of increased purchases by mutual funds. Lower-grade borrowers are finding it easier than ever before to tap capital market sources for funds, thereby reducing their reliance on banks.

Most important among the forces that have conspired to diminish the role of banks as primary sources of liquidity and credit is a new wave of stifling government regulation. In the wake of the late 1980s savings and loan debacle, Congress was determined that commercial banks not follow suit. It cost approximately $150 billion of taxpayers' money excluding interest to pay off the depositors of insolvent savings and loan associations, and the last thing either Congress or the embattled regulators of banking institutions wanted to see was for banks to follow with a full-blown crisis of their own. Accordingly, regulators toughened bank capital requirements and strengthened loan-risk criteria used in separating good loans from bad ones. In order to meet these tougher capital requirements, many banks simply shrunk their deposit and asset footings and watched their CD holders leave in droves.

To an increasing degree, banks today are focused on maximizing their profits rather than their market share. In this regard, banks are seeking the widest possible net interest margins between their cost of lendable funds and their earnings on loans and investments. Banks are also looking increasingly to fee income for activities such as the securitization of loans and the development and trading of off-balance-sheet items like interest rate and currency swaps.

The explosion of mutual funds, combined with financial innovation, have been the crucial factors in the striking eclipse of banks as a source of liquidity and as a provider of credit to consumer and business borrowers. During the decade of the 1980s and into the 1990s, the most attractive opportunities for individual investors have been the wide array of investment vehicles offered by mutual funds. To be sure, mutual funds have been around for some time. But during the past decade or so, the growth of mutual funds has been the most spectacular in their history.

In competing for investors, mutual funds have a fundamental advantage over banks in the form of lower fixed costs. Banks are stifled by over-regulation and too many buildings, pillars, marble, and layers of management. At their peak in influence in the mid-1970s there were about 14,000 banks around the country but failure, merger and consolidation have reduced this number to less than 11,000 at present. Mutual funds typically operate, in stark contrast, in tightly cramped offices with banks of telephones manned by a small but highly productive work force. Of course, mutual funds also have asset managers along with research and operations staffs, but these are also spartan compared with the bloated bank work force. Primarily for this reason, money market mutual funds consistently pay investors a higher return than comparable bank instruments. Of course, the higher yield offered by money market mutual funds is also required to compensate for the fact that they are not government insured, as are bank deposits.

CREDIT CRUNCHES (OLD AND NEW)

Banks introduced the negotiable CD in the early 1960s which grew to become a major source of liquidity for large institutional depositors in the 1960s and 1970s. At the same time, banks provided the lion's share of liquidity for more passive small investors during this period. For individuals, banks proved during this earlier period to be a convenient and safe place to build up their savings nest egg. Moreover, financial innovation and convenient alternative financial market investments had not yet reached the point of serving as viable alternatives for individuals with money to put to work.

All this has changed in the past decade or so as mutual funds have finally hit their stride. Today, mutual funds number roughly 5000 (more than the number of stocks listed on the New York Stock Exchange) and have assets of more than $2 trillion, doubling in size since 1990 alone. Now there is growing competition among mutual funds for individual investors' money as well as between mutual funds and commercial banks.

The old-fashioned credit crunches of the 1960s and early 1970s were quite predictable. These more traditional credit crunches became the major channel through which monetary policy operated to influence the economy. The "old-fashioned" credit crunch occurred precisely because of Regulation Q ceilings imposed by the Fed on bank time deposit rates. Banks could not raise their time deposit rates above these officially imposed ceilings, even if Fed credit-tightening actions had pushed interest rates on competing money market investments to higher and more attractive levels. You could start looking for a credit crunch when Fed moves to tighten the availability of credit reached the point of pushing short-term money market interest rates above the regulatory ceilings on bank savings and time deposits. At this point, banks suffered massive bouts of disintermediation whereby depositors pulled funds out of their accounts and reinvested them in higher-yielding money market investments. Specifically, holders of saving and time deposits pulled their funds out of banks and thrifts and invested them in higher-yielding Treasury bills or commercial paper. Banks and other depository institutions suffering this outsized loss of deposit funds cut back immediately on mortgage lending. Since these depository institutions accounted for the lion's share of mortgage lending at that time, housing activity promptly ground to a halt, eventually pulling economic activity down with it.

These old-fashioned credit crunches took place in 1966–67, 1969–70, and 1973–74. The resulting downturn in the housing market was especially severe in the latter crunch and, in turn, contributed importantly to the recession which began in December 1973 and continued through March 1975. Likewise, the 1969–70 crunch contributed importantly to the recession that began in January 1970 and continued through November 1970.

The "old-fashioned" credit crunches came to an end in the 1970s. The "old-fashioned" crunches disappeared as banks developed more sophisticated liability management techniques involving Eurodollars and other nondomestic deposit liabilities. These alternative sources of lendable funds could be expanded and contracted in line with the ebb and flow of loan demands. Also, most importantly, the monetary authorities acted to eliminate Regulation Q ceilings on bank CDs in the 1970s.

More recently, a modern 1990s-style credit crunch helped push the economy into this decade's first recession. Rather than trickling down from Federal Reserve tightening actions, this new version of a crunch seemed to percolate from the bottom up. The main factor that caused banks to shut off new loan activity was the much greater attention banks began to receive from regulators. In response to the accusation that regulators' lax supervision caused the 1980s savings and loan (S & L) crisis, regulators clamped down on the banks, demanding higher capital requirements, increased deposit insurance premiums, and hounding them with increased regulatory oversight and scrutiny. To meet the tougher capital standards (imposed under the Basel Accord of 1988), banks had to increase their risk-based capital-asset ratios to a hefty 8%. But at the same time, with bank profits declining, their stock prices falling, and bad loan problems worsening, most banks found this to be the worst possible time to raise funds through equity offerings to meet tougher capital standards. Eventually, many banks found the only way out was to simply cut off new lending activities altogether. This abrupt cutoff in the supply of bank credit, in a sinister new version of a credit crunch, contributed importantly to the recession which began in August 1990 and continued through March 1991.

Banks' New Postrecovery Role

The 1990–91 recession was followed by a weak recovery, which remained fragile and uneven from roughly the spring of 1991 through the spring of 1993. Banks remained unusually reluctant to make new loans to businesses as the recovery plodded along largely because of unrelenting, aggressive regulation. At the same time, given an attractive net interest margin—largely reflecting the Fed's aggressive efforts to push short-term interest rates sharply lower— banks were content to build up their liquid investment holdings of U.S. government securities. In addition, large multinational banks placed greater emphasis on proprietary trading in global currencies and securities and dealing in derivatives like interest rate and currency swaps as a means of increasing their profitability.

Looking ahead, individual investors are unlikely to favor bank CDs relative to other investment options. To protect their net interest margins, banks are likely to continue to be quick to cut their CD rates when the Fed is easing credit and slow to raise their CD rates when the Fed is tightening credit.

In the future, the only force acting to counter the eclipse of the bank CD as a source of liquidity for individual investors is the factor of safety. The fact that the government insures bank time deposits (up to $100,000) appears attractive to individual investors when there is a growing shadow cast over some money market mutual funds or short-term government income funds due to their excessive use of risky derivatives to boost return. Specifically, some money market mutual funds have relied excessively on exotic derivatives such as mortgage derivatives and structured financial products to boost returns in 1993 when short-term interest rates were abnormally low. These particular money market funds suffered heavy losses in 1994 in the wake of the Fed's credit-tightening actions, which rendered their derivatives completely illiquid.

COMPETITIVE THREATS AND SECURITIZATION

Looking ahead, banks are likely to increasingly prefer hefty off-balance-sheet fee income from activities such as interest rate and currency swaps. By 1992, bank income from nonlending activities amounted to a hefty 42% of total revenues, nearly double the 24% share in 1981. Banks also seem destined to become increasingly involved in the powerful securitization process sweeping the financial markets. To an increasing extent, banks are content to originate new loans, repackage them, and then sell them off their balance sheets. A bank can securitize any loan that can be standardized as to terms, risk, and borrower creditworthiness. The securitization of these loans strengthens banks' capital positions by increasing their capital-asset ratios. Examples of loans used in securitization include mortgage loans and various loans to individuals for autos, mobile homes, boats, and even credit card receivables. In contrast, business loans remain more difficult to securitize, but early efforts in this direction are nevertheless underway.

In the future banks will face increased competition for their prized corporate loan business. Finance companies have been a competitive threat in the business loan area for some time. More recently, on June 16, 1994, CS First Boston, a leading securities firm, announced that it would begin originating large commercial loans in partnership with Credit Suisse. This announcement was significant in that it marked the first time a leading securities firm made plans to originate, structure, and syndicate loans for major borrowers on a continuing basis. The idea behind these new "junk loans" as distinct from "junk bonds" is that these Wall Street firms have no intention of putting their own capital at risk, but rather the aim of these investment bankers is to help themselves to some of the lush fees that banks had so long enjoyed from such business loan activities. Within a week of First Boston's announcement, Merrill Lynch & Co. followed with an announcement that it too would also start originating large commercial loans. Other securities firms competing with banks for corporate "junk" loans include Lehman Brothers, Inc., and Goldman Sachs & Company. As other securities firms encroach on this turf of commercial banks, we can expect to see many banks actually become overcapitalized, as they play a diminishing role relative to nonbank sources in the extension of credit.

The profoundly important securitization process, along with overregulation, have contributed to a dramatic decline in banks' share of total domestic nonfinancial debt to less than 35% at present from the already noted peak of about 55% in 1975. To an increasing extent, American businesses are borrowing directly from large nonbank investors through commercial paper and other debt obligations, or they are raising funds directly from venture capitalists. The information and technological revolutions have permitted a wide range of investors—including pension funds, hedge funds, mutual funds, insurance companies, and finance companies—to make their own evaluations regarding credit and market risk, thereby allowing these investors to lend directly to a host of borrowers that traditionally borrowed only from banks.

Of course, the failure of many banks and S & Ls in the 1980s also contributed to the declining depository institutions' share of total credit. Those institutions, which encountered financial difficulties owing primarily to bad loans in real estate, energy, developing countries, and agricultural sectors, were closed, sold, or merged out of existence.

CONTRACTING ROLE OF BANKS EXPANDS YOUR OPTIONS

The growth of the securitization process and the increasing role of the capital markets as sources of credit have resulted in a massive new array of investment vehicles available to you from nonbank sources. Either directly, or indirectly through mutual funds, you can invest out of your own pocket in money market funds, equities, mortgage-backed securities, asset-backed securities, "junk" bonds or any number of other types of debt obligations. As an investor, you will be offered a higher return for these new securities, but they also carry higher risk.

Now more than ever before, these new vehicles offer you a greater opportunity for a higher return. Now you have greater flexibility in shifting funds among your many investment options. The primary medium for this revolution in personal finance has been the mutual fund, offering research capabilities, along with low-cost, high-volume transactions and efficient hedging capabilities to allow you to shift effortlessly among your many investment options.

The upshot is that as an investor you face a new world of enticing options, but they are also more complex. They demand that you personally give more attention to the different types of investments, the performance of the mutual fund as the intermediary through which you invest, and the economic and government policy backdrop in order to achieve a higher return.

This glittering array of innovative financial market instruments poses a major obstacle to any future comeback of bank CDs as a significant source of liquidity in individual investors' portfolios. For any reasonably active individual investor, the myriad money market, bond, and stock investment choices in a typical mutual fund family is simply too good to pass up.

Moreover, you can increase your returns and reduce your risk in your modern investment portfolio if you key certain shifts among your money market, bond, and stock holdings to Fed policy shifts. For example, once the Fed begins a series of credit-tightening steps over a period of several months, you should sell all your long-term bonds and invest half the proceeds in safe and liquid 3-month Treasury bills and half in 5-year Treasury notes that offer a yield that can be 75–85% of that on long-term Treasury bonds but with only half the volatility (risk).

In an important way, the fate of the bank CD is also directly tied to Fed policy shifts. Fed moves to ease credit, for example, will push short-term interest rates lower, giving banks a quick excuse to lower CD rates. This will immediately encourage you to shift out of bank CDs into higher yielding money market mutual funds or into still-higher-yielding bond funds. Conversely, when the Fed moves to tighten credit and push short-term market rates higher, banks will be slow to raise their CD rates.

THE FUTURE OF BANKS AND YOUR MONEY

U.S. banks have returned to good financial health and, at long last, seem to be able and willing to meet increased loan demands associated with a strengthening economy. In particular, there has been a sharp pickup in business loan demand in 1994 (see Figure 7.2) as business working capital needs have risen in line with efforts to step up production in response to strengthening sales. Also, banks will continue to provide backup credit lines for companies like Woolworth, the large retailer, which encountered financial difficulties in 1994 and was forced to curtail its short-term borrowing in the commercial paper market. In addition, bank loans to individuals have risen impressively in 1994.

The bad news is that the still overregulated U.S. banks are unlikely to be at the forefront of imaginative and technologically advanced longer-term efforts to intermediate global flows of savings

Figure 7.2 **Bank Business Loans**

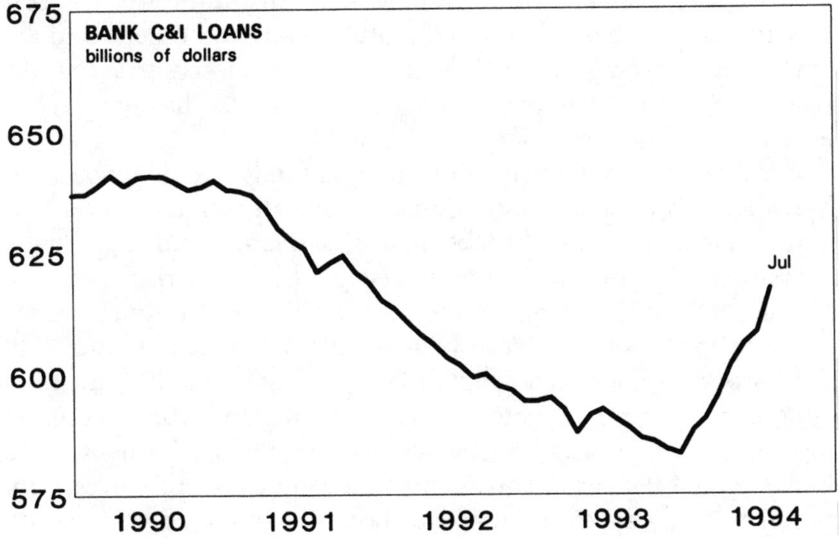

BANK C&I LOANS
billions of dollars

Source: Federal Reserve.

by channeling them into attractive and productive worldwide capital market investments. The less heavily regulated giant mutual fund families, hedge funds, insurance companies, and pension fund money managers all seem to have the upper hand on banks in this global intermediation process. This nonbank advantage is unlikely to be eroded any time soon, particularly given the gross government overregulation of traditional banking activities. In response, large banks have turned for profits to proprietary trading activities and to the huge fees associated with developing and trading derivative products such as interest rate swaps and currency swaps. Banks will also rely on other fee-based activities, including securitization, investment advice, securities custody, and processing activities.

Today, although still somewhat constrained by the Glass-Steagall Act, banks can establish discount brokerage services and sell mutual fund shares, along with other types of securities. As an investor you should keep an eye on this development, because it could mean that in the future you will get even better advice from banks on the credit risks of your investments. You may also find that the quality of money market mutual funds may improve as bank-sponsored funds compete more aggressively with more risky nonbank funds that seek to boost their returns through excessive reliance on risky derivatives. Most likely, future intensified competition between bank mutual funds and other mutual funds will also help to reduce management commissions. In the future, the best way to compare bank-sponsored mutual funds and others is to examine their earnings record and especially to closely examine the relative safety records of various nonbank funds that have relied excessively on derivatives to boost their returns.

Among the more imaginative mutual funds offered by banks is Wells Fargo's Lifepath mutual fund. It allocates its assets over several different categories (stocks, bonds, and cash), and it gradually shifts that allocation over time to reduce the fund's risk level. For instance, at the early stage in the lifepath this mutual fund initially takes greater risks to achieve higher returns, with an allocation of 54% stocks, 35% bonds, and 11% cash. But as the lifepath fund approaches the target date of the year 2020, the fund becomes more conservative with an ultimate asset mix of 15% stocks, 72% bonds, and 13% cash. This is just one example of the investment products banks have developed to become more competitive with securities firms.

A new trend is for banks to purchase money management firms and mutual fund companies. In recent acquisitions, Mellon Bank has bought the Boston Companies (money managers) and Dreyfus Corp., the nation's sixth largest mutual fund company. Also, PNC Bank Corp. has purchased Blackrock (money managers).

NEAR-TERM PROSPECTS FOR BOND AND STOCK INVESTMENTS

In 1994, you couldn't help but be shocked at how fast your investment fortunes can change. After a spectacular year in 1993, virtually every stock and bond mutual fund has reversed course and registered declines in total returns in the first half of 1994, in the wake of Fed actions to tighten the availability of credit. Over your morning cup of coffee you probably turned to your spouse and asked, "What is going on, what are we going to do? Should we move our money back into less risky bank CDs? Or is it better to stay in mutual funds, and shift money back and forth between bond, equity, and short-term money market funds?" Today, the answer is unquestionably the latter. But remember, there is no substitute for your scrutiny of the individual mutual funds' management, as well as of the economy and the Fed.

Basically, what you can expect to find in 1994 and 1995 is a major transition from an environment of slow growth and low inflation, which has been bullish for the stock and bond markets, to conditions of faster global growth and prospects for at least a moderate acceleration in inflation, which are bearish for stocks and bonds. The Fed has already responded to these new conditions by starting a series of gradual steps to tighten the availability of credit, which will exert upward pressure on short-term interest rates. Moreover, foreign central banks, including the Bank of England and the German Bundesbank, are likely to follow suit in tightening credit in 1995 as the European economic recovery gains momentum and begins to threaten future accelerating pressures. These conditions have already produced a U.S. bear market for bonds with long-term interest rates rising sharply. With interest rates rising, stocks may also encounter tougher sailing ahead.

MARKET CHOICES VERSUS BANK CDs

To end this chapter on the eclipse of the bank CD, it might be a good idea to take a systematic look at all new investment vehicles that you face and their general risk. This risk assessment combines the two major elements of risk, market risk and credit risk. Market risk is the risk that you will not be able to sell an asset promptly without significant loss of principal. Credit risk is the risk that the company issuing the securities will default on its interest and principal payments. Some securities may have no credit risk, others have high credit risk. All securities have at least some market risk. In Table 7.1, U.S. Treasury securities clearly have no credit risk, being backed by the full faith and credit of the U.S. government, but have some market risk. This nets out to a "low" overall risk profiling the comparison of investment vehicles below. Alternatively, in the case of mortgage-backed securities, credit risk tends to be low but market risk under some conditions can be extremely high, netting out to "high" overall risk. The "very high" risk profile applies to foreign debt and equities as well as derivatives. For foreign debt, default risk can be fairly high, but market risk may be at times extremely high. For complex structured note derivatives,

Table 7.1 **Comparison of Investment Vehicles**

	Risk Profile				
	Low	Medium	High	Very High	Comments
U.S. Treasury securities Bills Notes Bonds	X				Extremely safe
Government-sponsored agency securities	X				Safe
U.S. corporate debt Commercial paper Bonds		X			Fairly safe
Municipal (tax-exempt) bonds		X			Fairly safe
U.S. equities			X		Good bet
Foreign debt				X	Wild bet
Foreign equities				X	Wild bet
Mortgage-backed securities			X		Keep on guard
Asset-backed securities			X		Keep on guard
Derivatives				X	Beware

Source: Aubrey G. Lanston & Co. Inc.

default risk is not insignificant and market risk can at times be extremely high.

When you choose among a wide variety of investment vehicles, remember that you can boost your return while limiting your portfolio's overall risk if you diversify. For example, you might pick an item from each risk performance category in building your portfolio. Specifically, you might choose one "low"-risk vehicle such as government-sponsored agency securities, one "medium"-risk vehicle such as corporate debt (or tax-exempt municipals if you are in a high tax bracket), one "high"-risk vehicle such as U.S. equities, and perhaps one "very-high"-risk vehicle such as foreign equities. Just remember that after you have assembled all the different pieces of this portfolio, you must continue to monitor background political and economic conditions and the Fed closely.

8

Reaping Rewards
(or Cutting Your Losses)
from Exchange Rate Fluctuations

A major feature of the 1980s financial market revolution is global integration. In a shrinking world, you and your fellow investors can invest globally with greater ease and more promise than ever before. But along with these new investment opportunities carrying potentially higher returns comes more risk. In particular, you face not only the twin credit and market risks of the new unfamiliar foreign investments themselves, but you must also cope with currency risk. The unforeseen fluctuations in the U.S. dollar relative to the currency of the country in which you are investing can easily wipe out your profits on foreign investments. For instance, despite high indicated returns on stock or bond investments in a particular country, a sudden, unforeseen plunge in that country's currency relative to the dollar, if not adequately hedged, could promptly wipe out all your profits.

The foreign exchange value of the U.S. dollar is significantly influenced by the actions of the Fed in relation to those of other major foreign central banks. If, for example, the Fed is perceived as being less rigorous in its anti-inflation tightening actions than the German central bank (Bundesbank), then, other things being equal, the dollar is likely to decline in terms of the German D-mark. This requires that you be not only a diligent Fed watcher, but also a close observer of the Bundesbank and other major foreign central banks.

One of the advantages of investing through a global mutual

fund is that you can benefit from its management and research expertise in dealing with currency risk. Nevertheless, you must do your own homework as well in choosing a global mutual fund with a good earnings record. You should also make sure that your fund is not taking on more currency risk than you think is appropriate, given the ever-present threat of unforeseen foreign exchange fluctuations. In the final analysis, there is simply no substitute for learning more about economic and political conditions in countries in which you plan to invest.

As this book is going to press in the fall of 1994, the three-and-a-half-year-old U.S. recovery has reached an advanced stage of development, and U.S. bonds have entered a bear market phase as inflation fears heighten and the Fed takes a series of countering restrictive actions. At the same time, the declining dollar has been a major source of financial market instability. When the dollar falls in terms of the currencies of our major trading partners, there is the threat of rising U.S. import prices, which will, in turn, boost general inflationary pressures and expectations. At the same time, dollar weakness will cause foreign investors to dump unattractive dollar-denominated bonds, thus reinforcing upward pressure on U.S. long-term interest rates and adding to financial instability. Rising bond yields, in turn, are depressing already lofty U.S. equity prices.

In contrast, other major industrial countries such as Germany and Japan, which have lagged behind the United States in their respective recoveries, provide greater opportunities for successful bond and stock investment. And, of course, there is always the lure of high investment returns in the emerging economies of the Pacific Rim and Latin America.

As you evaluate the potential returns available overseas, it's important to factor in the cost of getting into and out of foreign securities, along with the foreign exchange risk. These entry and exit fees could easily cost you 5% of your returns, even before you pay the cost of hedging in order to neutralize the effects of currency fluctuations. Furthermore, if you seek to avoid the cost of hedging, the slumping dollar could someday surprise you by reversing course and strengthening in terms of the other major currencies. In that case your returns on foreign bond and equity investments would erode rapidly. Thus, as an individual investor with overseas exposure, you must give some attention to what is happening to the dollar and to the currency risk of the countries in which you are investing.

Monitoring fluctuations in foreign exchange rates is not necessarily just a defensive tactic. You also can stand to profit from this volatility. Specifically, you can profit under conditions when the dollar is under downward pressure, owing perhaps to persistently large U.S. trade deficits or declining confidence in the presiding administration's effectiveness. In these circumstances of a declining dollar, you would profit from heavier investment in foreign stocks and bonds. Not only would you benefit in this case from the actual return (price appreciation plus interest and dividends) on your foreign bond and stock investments, but also by the appreciation in the foreign currencies in which these investments are denominated.

In contrast, if it appears that the dollar may be about to reverse course and strengthen, perhaps reflecting aggressive Fed anti-inflation moves to tighten credit and push U.S. interest rates to more attractive levels relative to foreign interest rates, you should promptly lighten up on your foreign investments and pump the money into U.S. stocks and bonds.

Of course, you can also make relatively low-cost bets on the direction of the U.S. dollar in terms of foreign currencies by trading foreign currency options or futures themselves. For example, if you think the U.S. dollar is going to appreciate relative to the German D-mark, you can buy through your broker a put option on the D-mark. Conversely, if you think the dollar is going to decline, you buy a call option on the D-mark.

UNDERSTANDING FOREIGN EXCHANGE

Simply speaking, foreign exchange is the currency of foreign countries. You need to worry about it because investing in foreign stocks and bonds is becoming an increasingly important way to diversify portfolio risk. It can help to spread your risk because you can purchase stocks and bonds in countries that are at a different stage of economic recovery than the United States. Let's say that the U.S. economy, after a long period of recovery, is on the verge of contracting, while the German economy is lagging behind the United States and is just beginning its recovery. In that case, you might choose to take some of your assets out of the U.S. equity market and reinvest them in German stocks. In order to buy German stocks or bonds, you (or your mutual fund) need to exchange U.S. dollars for German D-marks. Conversely, when you eventually sell your German stocks or bonds, you must convert the proceeds from these sales of foreign securities back into U.S. dollars. In both instances, you are opening yourself up to foreign exchange risk.

Foreign exchange risk is the probability that the value relationship between two currencies will shift, and you will lose money as a consequence. The relationship between currencies is reflected in the foreign exchange rate, which for our purposes represents the terms of conversion between the U.S. dollar and some foreign currency. For instance, the dollar-yen foreign exchange rate is currently about 100, meaning 1 dollar can buy 100 Japanese yen. Alternatively, the dollar–D-mark exchange rate is about 1.55, meaning one U.S. dollar will buy 1.55 German D-marks. You can use exchange rates to guide your investment decisions. For instance, when the dollar is weakening in terms of foreign currencies, you should buy more foreign bonds and stocks. In contrast, when the dollar is strengthening in terms of foreign currencies you should buy more U.S. bonds and stocks.

PORTFOLIO DIVERSIFICATION INTO FOREIGN SECURITIES

Diversifying your portfolio into foreign bonds and stocks is a particularly appealing strategy in periods when major industrial economies around the world are growing at widely differing rates. At those times, look for early bull markets in either emerging or developed markets, where stock prices have not yet risen to overbought levels. For example, in Britain and other European economies, where recovery started much later than in the United States, the equity markets are poised for greater gains. Furthermore, Japan, which is lagging behind Europe in recovering from a deep and long recession, may provide still better equity investment opportunities. Europe and Japan also enjoy better political stability than that found in Mexico, Brazil, Argentina, and other emerging markets, where returns might be higher but are also much more volatile (risky).

INVESTING THROUGH MUTUAL FUNDS

One relatively efficient way to gain foreign exposure is through mutual funds. Not only does this approach require a smaller time investment, but also mutual fund managers have stronger negotiating clout and can arrange for much lower fees for foreign exchange transactions and hedging services. In addition, your mutual fund manager can tap a big reservoir of research on foreign countries and companies that would be beyond your reach as an individual investor.

Mutual funds can lend foreign exposure to your portfolio in several ways. For starters, certain "domestic" funds can act like a foreign account if they hold the stocks of large multinational corporations—such as Coca-Cola and Exxon—where a significant portion of the company's income comes from its overseas subsidiaries. Looking for that sort of fund is, perhaps, one of the more conservative ways to add foreign exposure to your portfolio. Another approach is to invest through so-called "global" mutual funds where stocks are purchased from all over the world, including the United States. Examples of some prominent global funds are Merrill Global AllocB and Templeton World Fund. Finally, representing a more volatile type of fund, there are "international" mutual funds that invest only outside the United States. Examples of the leading international funds include T. Rowe Price International Stock and Scudder International Fund. No matter which sort of mutual fund you choose, it's important that you take responsibility for following the exchange rate and make sure that your holdings make sense in light of global economic conditions.

FOREIGN STOCKS DON'T GUARANTEE DIVERSIFICATION

Striking a more cautious chord, you should note that during periods of pronounced global financial market volatility there has been a tendency of *all* domestic and foreign bond and equity markets to move together, especially to the downside. This phenomenon was vividly demonstrated in the period following the Fed's initial tightening step on February 4, 1994. Despite the wide divergence among their economic growth rates, the major bond and equity markets in the United States, Germany, Britain, Japan, and most emerging countries all slumped at the same time. Remarkably, this sharp drop in equity prices even extended to previously hot growth areas such as the Pacific Rim and Latin America.

Of course, domestic and foreign markets do not always move in concert. To a large extent, the February 1994 experience undoubtedly reflected the prompt unwinding of huge worldwide leveraged positions in stocks and bonds held by hedge funds, pension funds, and other large institutional investors. Following the Fed's initial tightening move and the ensuing sell-off, lenders such as brokers and banks forced these global speculators to meet margin calls, triggering further heavy selling. Ironically, the Fed's 25 earlier moves to increase credit availability, from June 1989 through September 1992, followed by an unusually prolonged period of Fed accommodation, triggered massive institutional investors' leveraged speculation in bonds and equities on a *worldwide* scale, which, in turn, ultimately destabilized the U.S. securities markets. Their emergence also rocked foreign bond and equity markets. Overseas markets were overwhelmed by the large flow of capital brought by this new breed of global speculator. And, in turn, they shuddered when that flow of liquidity was suddenly shut off and then reversed in response to the U.S. central bank's tightening step.

The main point for you to remember is that you can't count on foreign stock and bond investments to automatically diversify your investment portfolio. Most ominously, the evidence suggests that when there is a negative shock to the U.S. and foreign bond and stock markets such as the Fed's February 4, 1994, tightening action, the prices of U.S. and foreign stocks and bonds will tend to decline together. The upshot is that if you anticipate extreme global financial volatility, you should be prudent in limiting the percentage of your investment portfolio devoted to foreign investments to no more than 20%. This is only about half the maximum 40% percent for foreign stocks and bonds that investment advisors have recommended for your portfolio for purposes of diversification under more stable global financial market conditions.

HOW A WEAK DOLLAR DEPRESSES
YOUR STOCK AND BOND HOLDINGS

In order to be a savvy investor, you must always take the dollar into account. Even if your portfolio is confined only to domestic bond and stock holdings, dollar volatility may directly affect your fortunes. For example, if a U.S.-Japan trade dispute or other similar conflicts should suddenly push the foreign exchange value of the dollar lower in terms of the Japanese yen, and this weakness spreads to other major currencies and is expected to persist, foreign investors can be expected to dump unattractive dollar-denominated bonds on the market, thereby exerting upward pressure on U.S. long-term interest rates. If this upward pressure on long-term interest rates persists, investors are likely to shun stocks. Also operating to reduce the attractiveness of stocks in this situation is the likelihood that higher long-term interest rates will depress economic activity and weaken earnings growth. Thus, there is usually a chain reaction in which a declining U.S. dollar will lead to declining U.S. bond prices (rising yields) *and* declining U.S. stock prices.

In a recent bout of dollar weakness, the first hints of the dollar's sickening slide and its concomitant depressive effect on the financial markets came in August 1993. A new Japanese government rejected the Clinton administration's proposals for a type of quota system that would set numerical targets on the amount of foreign goods and services crossing Japanese borders. Foreign exchange traders saw this trade policy friction between the United States and Japan as a signal to sell the dollar and buy the Japanese yen, causing a marked slide in the U.S. currency. The slide was exacerbated by the release of reports showing an unexpectedly large trade deficit in the U.S. merchandise account and by a Clinton administration policy to talk the dollar lower in order to try to force the Japanese to open their markets to foreign goods and services thereby reducing the Japanese trade surplus. Subsequently, the Clinton administration tried to change course and shore up the dollar in order to counter growing market perceptions that it wanted the dollar lower (Japanese yen higher) in order to reduce the U.S. trade deficit with Japan by increasing the cost of Japanese exports to U.S. buyers. However, the Clinton administration did not make a sustained effort to support the dollar, leaving foreign exchange market traders relentlessly bearish on the dollar.

At times, the relationship between two currencies can have a spillover effect on other currency relationships. Look at what happened in April 1994, for instance. At this time, the dollar plunged in relationship to the yen, and most ominously, the dollar weakness spread to the relationship between the dollar and the German D-mark. The dollar's broadening weakness reflected, in addition to a continuing large trade deficit, a general loss of confidence in President Clinton: concerns abounded concerning the President's handling of foreign affairs and fear that the Whitewater scandal might impair his ability to govern effectively.

Exchange rate volatility can also impact the bond market. On Friday, May 2, 1994, the dollar's downward spiral was beginning to unsettle the bond market as participants feared that further dollar declines would induce more foreign investors to dump dollar-denominated bonds. The resulting spurt in long-term interest rates caught the Clinton administration's attention and the Treasury directed the Fed to intervene heavily in support of the dollar. Subsequently, on Wednesday, May 4, there was massive coordinated intervention in support of the dollar by no less than 16 central banks. In a major shift in Clinton administration dollar policy, Treasury Secretary Bentsen declared that "this Administration sees no advantage in an undervalued currency." The treasury secretary went on to observe that "recent movements in exchange markets have gone beyond what is justified by economic fundamentals."

The negative impact of the declining dollar on bond market psychology was also evident in the stock market. In some ways you could look at the stock market as taking its cues from the bond market. Specifically, the dollar broke into full retreat after the February 11, 1994, breakdown in trade talks between the United States and Japan. In the wake of this dollar decline, long-term bond yields shot up to 7.75% in early May from roughly 6.5% around the time of the breakdown in the trade talks. In turn, investors viewing a 7.75% yield on 30-year bonds found stocks relatively unattractive. The bottom line was that rising bond yields operated to push stock prices decidedly lower.

The basic message is that you must take foreign exchange conditions into account when managing your portfolio. Even if you do not hold foreign bonds or equities, you need to keep a watchful eye on the foreign exchange value of the dollar. If the dollar plunges sharply in terms of the Japanese yen, the German mark, or other major currencies, foreign investors will dump dollar denominated bonds, pushing bond yields to higher and more attractive levels relative to alternative stock investments. Here are some early warning signals that point to an impending dollar slump:

- The monthly U.S. trade deficit is increasing.
- U.S.-Japanese trade negotiations are hitting snags.
- Foreign central banks are hiking their official interest rates, thereby increasing the attractiveness of interest rates on foreign securities relative to those on U.S. dollar–denominated securities.

If you see these conditions on the horizon, you need to protect yourself by finding a safe haven, preferably in short-term liquid investments in one of the strengthening currencies.

To sum up, we've seen that the Fed has an important influence on the dollar and, moreover, that the federal government's trade policies can also play a major role in influencing the dollar. The Fed can clearly have a positive impact on the dollar by tightening credit and increasing interest rates on dollar-denominated securities to more attractive levels relative to interest rates on foreign securities. In contrast, a misguided U.S. government trade policy that seeks to force Japan to open its markets to foreign goods and services by talking the dollar down will lead to an unstable dollar, which, in turn, leads to unstable financial markets.

MANAGING EXCHANGE RATE VOLATILITY

Exchange rate relationships are by their very nature volatile and unpredictable. The best bet, particularly if you are a conservative investor, is to at least partially hedge your currency value exposure on foreign investments so that exchange rate volatility will not eat up your total returns on foreign bonds and equities. Of course, the cost of hedging foreign exchange risk prunes some of your potential gains from investing in undervalued stocks and bonds.

To try to negate the impact of unpredictable currency fluctuations on your foreign bond and stock investments, you can use currency futures to lock in a certain exchange rate. In essence, you are hedging currency risks in order to concentrate on the identification of good foreign stocks and bonds to buy. But you must remember that hedging costs money, which lowers the ultimate return on your foreign investments.

Here are foreign currency nonhedging and hedging examples:

1. *Nonhedging.* Let's say you are an American investor who wishes to buy a German bond yielding 7.75%. Assume that you leave the foreign exchange risk in this transaction unhedged. But immediately after you exchange U.S. dollars for German D-marks to purchase $160,000 worth of the German bonds, the U.S. dollar unexpectedly begins to strengthen in terms of the German D-mark from 1.5320 at the time of the purchase of the German bonds to 1.6320 exactly one year later when you decide to sell the German bonds. This unforeseen appreciation of the U.S. dollar in terms of the German D-mark causes a 6.6% foreign exchange loss in your German bond, nearly offsetting your entire initial 7.75% annual yield. (This example assumes no change in the price of German bonds during the year in which you held them; in fact, the dollar's appreciation in terms of the German D-mark assumed in this example might have resulted in a decline in the price of your German bonds, thus adding a capital loss on your German bond holdings to your foreign exchange loss.

2. *Hedging.* To hedge your German bond investment, you sell through a broker two German D-mark futures contracts on the Chicago Mercantile Exchange covering 125,000 D-marks per contract. (You owe $1000 margin per contract, or a total of $2000 to be redeemed when the trade is unwound.) Assuming the U.S. dollar strengthens from 1.5320 to 1.6320 D-marks during the course of the 12 months you intend to hold the German bonds, you will make $10,650 on the sale of the D-mark futures contracts. In contrast, your exchange rate loss on the German bond investment, assuming the dollar appreciates from 1.5320 to 1.6320 D-marks, would have been $10,564. The total cost of this near-perfect hedge is only about $100, consisting of $40 commission ($20 per round turn) and $60 (opportunity cost of lost interest forgone on $2000 tied up in margin until the trade is unwound).

The bottom line is that in this case of an unforeseen appreciation in the U.S. dollar, the 7.75% yield which attracted you to German bonds in the first place is nearly completely wiped out if your currency transaction is unhedged and the dollar unexpectedly strengthens in terms of the German D-mark during the year that you plan to hold the German bond, whereas your return is preserved if you use proper hedging techniques by selling foreign currency futures contracts to offset your exchange rate exposure.

REAPING REWARDS FROM
EXCHANGE RATE FLUCTUATIONS

As a way of reaping benefits from exchange rate fluctuations, you should follow some common-sense rules. For example, you should avoid investing in countries with extremely volatile currencies. (An extremely volatile currency might, for example, experience recurring fluctuations of 10% or more per month in terms of the U.S. dollar.) Also, you should avoid investing in stocks and bonds in countries where exchange controls are either in place or threatened. You can find out from your bank whether a country has imposed exchange controls on the inflow or outflow of investment funds. The unexpected imposition of exchange controls in a country where you have invested funds can cause major declines in prices of stocks and bonds in that country. For example, when Spain was forced by the European currency crisis to impose exchange controls in September 1992, its stock prices fell to the lowest levels since the crash of 1987. The danger signals you should watch for that precede foreign exchange controls are such things as massive foreign exchange speculation against the affected currency or chronic balance of payments deficits in the affected country. Such conditions cause the flight of desperately needed hard currency out of the affected country.

As a rule, you should avoid investing in the securities of countries experiencing extreme political instability. Instead, you should seek out countries with sufficient political stability to promote sustained noninflationary economic growth. You are looking for a country capable of generating adequate domestic savings to finance private and public investment demands. Most important, you want to invest in a country with a central bank that is sufficiently independent of government political influence to pursue the primary objective of a sound currency.

Whether you are investing indirectly through mutual funds, as is generally preferred in the case of foreign investments, or directly in the global financial markets, you should read carefully *The Wall Street Journal* and other publications like *Barron's* to determine the investment patterns of the new institutional investor powerhouses such as hedge funds, pension funds, and other large global money managers. Specifically, you should watch for major shifts in investment patterns by these big global institutional investors, as, for example, when they bet on big rallies in European debt and equity markets in second half of 1993 and the first half of 1994. The idea was that since the European recovery was lagging the U.S. economic recovery by at least two years, there was still room for appreciation in those foreign bond and stock markets. It was also hoped that the German Bundesbank and other European central banks would follow the Fed's earlier example and ease aggressively, but these hopes were never completely realized. In the future, you should also watch closely for shifts by these new institutional investor powerhouses out of financial assets like stocks and bonds into real assets like gold, oil, or commodities.

Section Four

MANAGING YOUR INVESTMENTS SUCCESSFULLY

*N*ow that you know how important the Federal Reserve's actions are to your financial welfare, you might find yourself rethinking your earlier investment decisions and, indeed, your whole portfolio. In any case, whether you are starting out or whether you are a veteran of the financial markets, this section will show you how to use your understanding of the Fed to protect your principal and achieve higher returns.

As you contemplate your new investment approach founded on Fed policy shifts, you need to think first about how you can adjust your investment portfolio in a way that uses your knowledge to your best advantage. This section will give you the key to success. The idea is to make a few major adjustments in your holdings of cash, stocks, and bonds from time to time, triggered by certain significant Fed policy shifts. To help you anticipate these Fed policy shifts, you need to be aware of economic turning points and what is happening to general inflationary pressures.

This section will reveal four cardinal rules that can help guide your investment strategy. For example, when the economy slips into recession, wait until the Fed responds with at least three consecutive steps to increase the availability of credit within any given year and then shift your entire portfolio into approximately one-half to one-third long-term (30-year) Treasury bonds and half to two-thirds stocks. You should take care not to let cash accumulate in your portfolio during these periods. Once the economy finally reverses course and begins to recover, you should continue to hold onto your balanced portfolio—although there can be an important difference in the types of stocks and bonds therein—so long as inflationary pressures remain dormant and the Fed continues to maintain an accommodative policy stance. (The huge 1993 bond and stock market rallies took place in these conditions.)

You will also learn how to anticipate market downturns. You will find out how to recognize early-warning signals of inflation such as a general increase in commodity prices, inventory accumulation triggers, and accelerating credit growth, thus uncovering the best investing strategy in an inflationary environment.

This section is a must for all investors seeking a successful asset allocation plan. You get down to the nuts and bolts of investing, including a detailed look at your mutual fund investment options. You learn what specifically to look for in choosing a mutual fund. Remember that all this attention given to mutual funds is not intended to imply that you should not invest directly in some investments, particularly U.S. Treasury debt obligations, rather than indirectly through mutual funds.

To be a safe as well as a profitable investor, you must also be aware of the potholes in your portfolios. In particular, you should comb your investment holdings for derivatives that can become extremely illiquid in the wake of shocks such as the Fed's move on February 4, 1994, to tighten credit for the first time in five years. (Derivatives are complex financial instruments whose value is based on, or derived from, underlying assets.)

Above all, this section provides your investment bread and butter. It offers specific clues of successful investing tied to Fed policy actions. Just remember two critical elements in your investment approach. First, portfolio balance and diversification are major keys to individual investor success. Second, we have found that you can achieve enhanced returns with less risk by adjusting your portfolio holdings to coincide with Fed actions. This section will show you how to master this strategy.

9

Cashing In on the Explosion in Mutual Funds

Over the past three years, you probably made the most important shift of your life in your asset holdings, from bank CDs to stocks, bonds, and other investments. And if you're like most people, after going through a period of evaluating your investments, you probably shifted a significant portion of your investment nest egg into one or more of the hot new mutual fund portfolios. Actually, once you finally decided to make the move, you were probably impressed by how easy and cheap it was to take it. All it took was a phone call to the toll free number of a mutual fund.

THE RISE OF MUTUAL FUNDS

If you shifted your holdings from CDs to mutual funds, you were not alone. In fact, mutual funds are overtaking banks. Banks have traditionally been the major repositories of household wealth as well as suppliers of capital to small- and medium-sized companies, but now mutual funds are threatening to take over this role. In 1993, as Table 9.1 shows, net mutual fund assets totaled $2 trillion, which is equivalent to nearly 70% of bank deposits, up from only 10% of bank deposits a decade earlier. Recent industry surveys estimate that in 1993 upwards of one-third of all U.S. households owned shares in a mutual fund, compared to only 6% in 1980.

Mutual funds have not only begun to overshadow banks, they are also gathering clout in the equity, bond, and tax-exempt securi-

Table 9.1   **Net Assets of Mutual Fund Industry, by Fund Type, End of Period, Selected Years, 1960–1993**

(Billions of Dollars)

Period	Stock	Bond	Money Market[1]	Total
1960	11.9	5.1	N.A.	17.0
1965	25.2	10.0	N.A.	35.2
1970	38.5	9.1	N.A.	47.6
1975	32.4	9.8	3.7	45.9
1980	41.0	17.4	76.4	134.8
1985	116.9	134.8	243.8	495.5
1990	245.8	322.7	498.4	1066.9
1991	367.6	440.9	539.6	1348.1
1992	475.4	580.9	543.6	1599.9
1993	749.0	761.1	565.3	2075.4

[1]Taxable and tax-exempt.
N.A. – Not available.
Source: Investment Company Institute.

ties markets (see Table 9.2). In 1993, mutual funds were the largest purchaser of equities and the second largest purchaser of bonds, next to insurance companies. Their emergence as a major player has had an influence on the structure, volatility, and products offered in these markets. For example, reflecting growing mutual fund purchases, there has been a fourfold increase in the number of stock initial public offerings (IPOs) from 150 in 1990 to 571 in 1993.

The explosion in mutual funds has also had an impact on the financial outlook of yourself, your family, and your friends. As more of you enter the financial markets through mutual funds, your financial worth has become more volatile. Rather than having your assets stowed away in safe bank CDs with their low, yet predictable, rates of return, you are now experiencing the greater highs and lows of the stock and bond markets. This changes your reaction to economic news such as a Fed rate increase. Now you will react to the news with concern not only if you're a potential home buyer because of a potential backup in mortgage rates, but also because of the negative impact of bond or stock market declines on your wealth, or net worth position.

From a political standpoint, it is little wonder, given the spectacular growth and popularity of mutual funds among his constituents, that President Bill Clinton has become so sensitive to bond and stock market developments. The emphasis that Treasury

Table 9.2 **Distribution of New Purchases of Equities, Corporate Bonds, and Tax-Exempt Securities, by Type of Investor, Selected Years, 1980–1993[1]**
(*Billons of Dollars*)

Type of Investor	1980	1982	1984	1986	1988	1990	1991	1992	1993	Memo Level, 1993
Equities										
Mutual funds[2]	−1.8	3.5	5.9	20.2	−16.0	14.4	44.6	67.2	129.5	667.3
Closed-end funds	−1.2	−0.7	−0.5	3.0	0.6	0.7	0.3	−1.0	−0.9	20.4
Households[3]	−11.5	−31.8	−70.1	−135.2	−101.0	−27.2	−22.8	−5.7	−76.0	3204.5
Depository	−0.6	−0.5	−0.3	0.9	0.4	−4.0	1.9	0.3	2.1	19.5
Insurance	3.5	5.1	−4.1	−2.4	0.2	−12.6	−5.6	11.6	35.0	279.5
Pension funds	21.8	28.0	2.5	26.7	13.8	2.3	29.0	11.3	4.4	1586.1
Foreign	4.2	3.7	−3.4	17.9	−2.9	−16.0	10.4	−5.8	20.4	320.6
Broker-dealers	0.1	0.9	−1.0	1.4	0.2	−3.3	2.4	−0.6	6.7	22.9
Total	14.5	8.2	−71.0	−67.6	−104.6	−45.8	60.2	77.3	121.2	6120.8
Bonds										
Mutual funds[2]	1.3	0.2	3.6	26.8	14.2	13.6	12.8	19.8	65.7	186.0
Closed-end funds	0	0.4	−0.4	1.4	9.4	−1.7	−1.9	1.9	0.8	15.4
Households[3]	−1.83	−2.2	−10.6	35.9	−29.9	18.3	26.2	−13.4	−38.7	122.3
Depository	7.1	6.1	17.0	30.5	23.9	−14.7	4.7	6.9	16.3	192.2
Insurance	8.8	15.7	27.9	54.9	79.3	65.7	36.2	59.6	71.3	823.0
Pension	23.3	13.7	28.1	30.4	36.5	26.6	43.4	46.8	33.0	494.5
Foreign	9.2	15.7	15.6	39.1	15.9	5.3	16.2	18.5	30.3	207.4
Broker-dealers	0.4	2.5	5.7	0.3	9.8	−4.0	12.0	10.0	22.2	73.0
Total	36.3	52.1	86.8	219.4	159.0	109.2	149.5	150.1	200.9	2113.8
Tax-exempt securities										
Mutual funds[4]	2.0	10.9	12.6	59.3	12.3	29.8	34.2	41.3	52.9	217.9
Closed-end funds	0	0	0	1.1	3.8	1.8	14.1	11.8	11.9	51.8
Households[3]	0.8	31.2	31.7	−2.8	50.4	34.1	44.1	11.1	−16.6	589.8
Depository	12.7	4.3	12.2	−28.7	−22.5	−16.0	−14.8	−6.1	2.1	101.7
Insurance	8.0	4.9	−3.2	15.6	7.8	5.5	−12.2	8.7	8.1	153.8
Other[5]	0.5	1.8	5.4	1.3	2.0	2.2	4.2	−1.0	1.0	38.5
Total	23.9	53.1	58.7	45.7	53.7	57.4	69.6	65.8	59.4	1153.5

[1]Annual rate.
[2]Excludes money market mutual funds.
[3]Includes nonprofit organizations and personal trusts administered by banks and nondeposit noninsured companies.
[4]Includes money market mutual funds.
[5]Pension funds, broker-dealers, nonfarm nonfinancial corporate business, and state and local government general funds.
Source: Federal Reserve Board, flow of funds accounts.

Secretary Bentsen and Fed Chairman Greenspan have placed on bond market reactions and cutting the deficit has caused Clinton to raise taxes and trim his plans for increased social investment (spending), to focus instead on cutting the deficit more deeply, so as to exert downward pressure on long-term bond yields. Also, global stock and bond market developments have appeared to have a significant influence on Clinton trade policies and other international initiatives. Moreover, when the 1996 presidential election year comes around, it is likely that the fate of the stock market will carry considerable weight on the election's outcome, given the high percentage of the population participating in the stock market directly or indirectly through mutual funds.

Assuming that you made the shift from bank CDs to bond or stock mutual funds sometime in 1991 or 1992, you had to feel like an investment genius, possibly the last of the big time Wall Street financiers. Things were so good in the bond and stock markets in 1993 that the average New Yorker riding the subway to work was reading the financial page of the newspaper instead of the obligatory sports page. These days, however, you might feel the urge to cancel your subscription to the daily newspaper that brings you 1994's bleak financial news and run to the nearest financial planners' office. Resist that urge. Although the financial markets have become more challenging of late, we will show you how to understand the fluctuations in your mutual funds' returns and how to bring them into line with your financial objectives.

ABCs of Mutual Funds

Let's take a moment to look more closely at the investment vehicle that has changed the financial and political landscape so dramatically. You and your fellow investors are attracted to mutual funds for a variety of reasons. Most important, mutual funds give you convenient access to a great variety of investment options. (The price of mutual fund shares, apart from brokerage commissions, equals the net asset value of the fund, determined by dividing the market value of the fund's assets, less any liabilities, by the number of outstanding shares.) Specifically, mutual funds are an effective means of diversifying your asset holdings into both domestic and foreign stocks and bonds. Furthermore, as an individual investor in mutual funds, you benefit from their extensive asset management and research capabilities. In addition, because of their high volume of transactions, mutual funds are a low cost means of executing securities sales and purchases and currency hedging operations.

Among the most important items you should look for in choosing a fund is a successful fund manager who has been with the fund for a considerable period of time. Also, you should examine the fund's earnings record during the preceding five years. In addition, it would be a good idea to check the fees charged by the fund and compare them with others. You should seek out domestic equity mutual funds with a ratio of expenses to total fund assets of 2% or less. For bond funds, the ratio of expenses to total fund assets should be 1% or less. Perhaps your best bet would probably be to choose one of the large mutual fund families (see Table 9.3) so as to be able to switch easily and cheaply between money, bond, and stock funds.

So, you might wonder, what are the disadvantages of holding mutual funds. To start with, mutual funds are more risky than bank CDs because they are neither insured by the government nor necessarily redeemable at par. In addition, some mutual funds may be making excessive use of high-risk derivatives in order to boost earnings. For instance, this was the case with several short-term government funds which sought to boost returns using risky mortgage derivatives and structured financial instruments in 1993, when short-term interest rates were abnormally low, and then suffered huge losses in 1994 on these illiquid derivative investments when interest rates spiked higher.

THE MUTUAL FUND MENU

One of the most attractive characteristics of mutual funds is their diversification. Each fund offers greater diversity than an equivalent purchase of a single stock. Also, you can increase the diversity of your portfolio by purchasing different types of funds. As more mutual funds are created and compete for the same market share, they each seek ways to distinguish themselves from their competitors. As a result, you'll find an array of very specialized mutual funds—such as Fidelity Select-Health Care, T. Rowe Price Science and Technology Fund, and Lexington Gold Fund.

Table 9.3   **Largest Stock Funds: Percentage Gains for Period Ended March 31, 1994; Assets as of December 31, 1993**

Stock Funds	Assets ($ millions)	Performance		
		1st Quarter	12 Months	5 Years
Fidelity Magellan Funds	$31,705.1	−1.60%	12.94%	117.25%
Investment Co. of America	19,005.0	−3.70	3.88	77.36
Washington Mutual Inv	12,638.5	−5.05	0.33	67.40
Vanguard Windsor	10,610.8	−1.80	7.67	59.64
Income Fund of America	10,338.9	−4.41	2.50	73.88
Janus Fund	9,199.6	−2.63	2.62	113.98
Fidelity Asset Manager	9,094.4	−4.84	10.53	92.72
Fidelity Puritan	8,988.2	−0.54	10.71	83.54
20th Century Ultra	8,362.4	−1.82	19.73	186.25
Vanguard Index 500	8,272.7	−3.84	1.29	75.38
Vanguard Wellington Fund	8,075.8	−3.86	3.74	62.16
Fidelity Growth & Income	7,684.0	−2.68	7.94	105.14
Vanguard Windsor II	7,616.3	−4.46	1.76	64.34
Fidelity Equity—Income	6,641.9	−3.25	7.77	65.34
Dean Witter Dividend Growth	6,549.6	−4.81	2.86	68.32
Fidelity Contrafund	6,193.3	−1.64	9.76	185.82
Europacific Growth	5,803.0	−0.72	26.27	93.89
Putnam Growth & Income A	5,327.0	−4.00	3.63	71.68
American Mutual	5,194.3	−3.22	3.86	69.09
New Perspective Fund	5,086.0	−1.73	19.62	88.59
Growth Fund of America	5,062.5	−2.51	10.58	84.95
Fidelity Equity—Income II	5,021.9	−1.43	7.99	N.A.
Templeton World	4,986.1	−0.64	23.14	71.76
Twentieth Century Select	4,938.0	−5.12	2.01	75.85
Merrill Global Alloc B	4,874.2	−0.15	11.62	95.14
AVERAGE STOCK FUND	−	−3.33	5.43	78.69
S&P 500 (w/dividends)	−	−3.79	1.46	76.97

N.A. − Not applicable; fund is too new
Source: Lipper Analytical Services. Reprinted by permission of the *Wall Street Journal* © 1994 Dow Jones & Co., Inc. All rights reserved worldwide.

Many investors avoid highly specialized mutual funds because they carry greater risk. This risk is evident in sector stock mutual funds such as health/biotech which were devastated by fears of excessive government interference, including possible price controls in this sector under the proposed Clinton Health Care Plan. Likewise, single-state muni funds, purchased to avoid paying certain state taxes, suffer from an inherent lack of national diversification, and thus carry a lot more risk than more geographically diversified muni funds.

Listed next are the main categories of equity, bond, and

money market mutual funds from which you can choose. These categories were developed by rating services such as Morningstar and Lipper Analytical Services. The rating services will assign individual mutual funds to these categories based on the investment focus described in the fund's prospectus and the actual investment practices of the fund.

U.S. Diversified Stock Mutual Funds

Small-Company Growth—Limit investment to small companies, but the definition of "small" varies. (Standard & Poor's has introduced a *small* Cap 600 index that includes stocks of companies that range in size from a market capitalization of $27 million to $886 million, with an average capitalization of $302 million.)

Mid-Cap—Consist of the stocks of middle-sized companies. (The Standard & Poor's Mid Cap 400 measures mid-sized companies with an average capitalization of $1.2 billion.)

Capital Appreciation—Try to achieve maximum capital appreciation in their equity investments through such means as high turnover, leveraging, and the use of options.

Growth—Invest in the stocks of companies with exceptional long-term records of earnings growth.

Growth and Income—Seek to balance their investments between the stocks of companies with good growth prospects and those with high dividend income.

Equity Income—Focus upon the stock of companies with high dividend income.

Sector Stock Mutual Funds

Technology—Invest at least 65% of their assets in science and technology stocks.

Financial Services—Invest at least 65% of their assets in stocks of financial service companies.

Health/Biotech—Invest at least 65% of their assets in health care, medical companies, and biotechnology companies.

Real Estate—Invest at least 65% of their assets in real estate company securities.

Environmental—Hold at least 65% of their assets in stock and convertible securities of companies contributing to a cleaner environment, such as waste management and pollution control companies.

Utilities—Invest at least 65% of their assets in the stocks of utility companies.

Natural Resources—Invest at least 65% (usually more) in natural resource stocks.

Gold—Place at least 65% of their assets in gold-mining companies, gold coins, or bullion.

International Stock Mutual Funds

Latin America—Consist mainly of securities trading on local exchanges in Mexico, Brazil, Argentina, Chile, and other Latin American countries.

Global Small Company—Invest at least 25% of their assets in small companies outside the U.S.

Global—Invest at least 25% of their assets in non-U.S. securities.

Pacific Region—Concentrate on stocks trading on the exchanges of one or more Pacific Basin countries.

Canada—Are limited mainly to securities that trade on Canadian exchanges.

International—Concentrate on securities traded outside the United States.

Japan—Are limited mainly to securities traded in Tokyo, or on exchanges in other major Japanese cities.

Europe—Consist mainly of securities traded on European exchanges.

Fixed-Income Mutual Funds

Municipal Bond Funds

General Muni—Invest at least 65% of their assets in municipal bonds carrying the top four credit ratings.

Insured Muni—Invest at least 65% of their assets in municipal bonds that have been insured by specialized insurers for timely payment of interest.

Intermediate Muni—Are limited to tax-exempt securities having an average maturity of 5–10 years.

High-Yield Muni—Invest at least 50% of their assets in low-rated tax-exempt securities.

Short-Term Muni—Are limited to tax-exempt securities having an average maturity of less than 5 years.

Single State Muni—Are confined to securities that are exempt from taxation in a particular state.

Taxable Fixed-Income Funds

Adjustable-Rate Mortgage—Invest at least 65% of their assets in adjustable-rate mortgage securities or other securities collateralized by or representing an interest in mortgages.

Short-Term U.S. Treasury—Invest at least 65% of their assets in U.S. Treasury bills, notes, and bonds with weighted maturities of less than 5 years.

Short-Term U.S. Government—Invest at least 65% of their assets in securities issued or guaranteed by the U.S. government or its agencies with weighted maturities of less than 5 years.

Intermediate U.S. Treasury—Invest at least 65% of their assets in U.S. Treasury notes and bonds with weighted maturities of 5–10 years.

Intermediate U.S. Government—Invest at least 65% of their assets in securities issued or guaranteed by the U.S. government or its agencies with weighted maturities of 5–10 years.

Short-Term Investment-Grade Debt—Invest at least 65% of their assets in debt rated in the top four grades with maturities averaging less than 5 years.

Intermediate Investment-Grade Debt—Invest at least 65% of their assets in debt rated in the top four grades with maturities averaging 5–10 years.

General U.S. Treasury—Invest at least 65% of their assets in U.S. Treasury bills, notes, and bonds.

General U.S. Government—Invest at least 65% of their assets in U.S. government and agency issues.

GNMA—Invest at least 65% of their assets in Government National Mortgage Association securities.

U.S. Mortgage—Invest at least 65% of their assets in mortgages or securities issued by the U.S. government and certain agencies.

Corporate Debt A Rated—Invest at least 65% of their assets in corporate debt rated A or better or in government securities.

Corporate Debt BBB Rated—Invest at least 65% of their assets invested in corporate issues rated in the top four grades or in government securities.

General Bond—No quality or maturity restrictions, but they keep the bulk of their assets in corporate and government debt issues.

High Current Yield—Invest assets mainly in corporate junk bonds and similar low-rated fixed-income securities offering high yields.

Short-World Multimarket Income—Are confined to nondollar and dollar fixed-income securities with a weighted maturity of less than 5 years.

General World Income—Are limited to nondollar and dollar fixed-income securities with no restrictions on maturities.

Short-Term Fixed-Income Funds

U.S. Treasury Money Market—Invest primarily in U.S. Treasury securities with average maturities of less than 70 days.

U.S. Government Money Market—Mostly confined to securities issued by or guaranteed by the U.S. government or its agencies with maturities averaging less than 70 days.

Money Market—Focus on high-quality corporate commercial paper and other securities rated in the top two grades with average maturities of less than 70 days.

Tax-Exempt Money Market—Are limited to high-quality municipal securities with average maturities under 70 days.

Combination Equity and Fixed-Income Mutual Funds

Convertibles—Are confined mostly to convertible bonds and preferred stock.

Balanced—Aim to preserve principal by investing about 60% of their assets in stock and about 40% in bonds.

Balanced Target—Aim to provide a guaranteed return of principal at maturity by investing a portion of their assets in zero coupon Treasury bonds and the remainder in long-term growth stocks.

Fixed Income—Invest at least 75% of their assets in fixed-income securities, such as bonds, preferred stocks, and money market instruments.

Flexible Income—Are confined primarily to bonds, convertibles, and common stocks and warrants, but with no more than 25% of their assets in common stocks.

As an investor you can use this mutual fund menu as a quick checklist of the options available to you. Remember that for fixed-income securities your options are basically short term (less than 5 years maturity), intermediate term (5–10 years maturity), and long term (more than 10 years maturity). For equities, your basic decisions are between domestic and foreign and between large, medium, and small capitalized (cap) companies. (A company's capitalization is calculated as its share price times the number of its shares outstanding.)

WEIGHING RISKS AND RETURNS

Before you select one or even several mutual funds, first you should contemplate your investment objective. Perhaps your investment objective is to earn 10% or more a year on your investment holdings as you approach retirement. Then you should decide on an investment approach. Are you looking for income, value, growth, or capital appreciation? What is your time horizon? What is the biggest loss you can stomach? Your responses to these questions will help you shape the proper investment balance between stocks and bonds, which, in turn, will help you build (or rebuild) a more profitable and coherent portfolio.

Many investors use mutual funds exclusively to meet their investment goals. How can you do that? Let's say that your objective is a return of 10% or more a year on your investment portfolio. You can use Table 9.4 to determine what your rough balance between equity and intermediate bond funds might have to be if you want to meet your objective of an annual average 10% or higher return. Note that for the entire post–World War II period from 1946 to 1993, you would have to hold upwards of 75% stock funds and 25% intermediate-maturity bond funds to achieve an average annual return of 10.5%. During this period of nearly 50 years, your worst one-year loss, if you held approximately 75% stock funds and 25% intermediate-maturity bond funds, would have been 18.4%.

Some financial advisors urge you to hold all equity funds. While it is true that over long periods of time, stock mutual funds will earn more than bond funds, it is also true that stock funds tend to be more risky than bond funds. You should think of bond funds as your security cushion. During the 1946–93 period, your average

Table 9.4 **Portfolio Risks Versus Rewards, 1946–1993**
Results for portfolio holding varying amounts of stocks and bonds.

	Portfolio	Number of Down Years	Average Loss in Down Year	Worst 1-Year Loss	Average Annual Return
Aggressvie	100% stocks	11	−9.4%	−26.5%	11.7%
Growth	75% stocks/ 25% bonds	9	−7.2	−18.4	10.5
Balanced	50% stocks/ 50% bonds	8	−4.0	−10.4	9.1
Income	75% bonds/ 25% bonds	5	−1.5	−2.7	7.6
Conservative	100% bonds	5	−0.7	−1.3	5.9

Note: Figures based on Ibbotson Associates data for the Standard & Poor's 500 stock index and intermediate-term government bonds.
Source: T. Rowe Price Associates Reprinted by permission of the *Wall Street Journal* © 1994 Dow Jones & Company, Inc. All rights reserved worldwide.

annual return if you held equity funds would have been 11.7%. But you had to have a strong stomach for risk. Otherwise you were destined to spend some sleepless nights as you contemplated when that next 26.5% worst-loss year might come.

A better idea for modern-day mutual fund investors with only moderate stomach for risk is to split their mutual fund holdings into, say, two-thirds to one-half stock funds and one-third to one-half fixed-income funds. Within your fixed-income securities funds you should take your cue from the Fed in making shifts between long-term bond funds and short-term fixed-income investments. Specifically, you should invest in long-term bond funds when the Fed is engaging in a series of credit-easing actions against the background of a weakening economy and declining inflationary pressures. Conversely, when the Fed is engaging in a string of credit-tightening actions to counter excessive economic growth and rising inflationary pressures, you should sell your long-term bond funds and invest the proceeds in short-term fixed-income investments.

Moreover, within your equity portfolio you should emphasize diversity. After determining your investment aim, you should invest in the diversified domestic equity funds that seek to realize your investment goal. In addition, you might invest a portion of your equity portfolio in foreign equity funds, particularly in situations such as in the 1991–94 period when recoveries in major foreign industrial economies were lagging behind recovery in the United States. As the U.S. stock market begins losing steam, emerging market funds such as a Latin America fund or the Pacific Rim fund may also be worth considering. But remember to carefully weigh the risks associated with these foreign equities before purchasing shares.

TOP 25 MUTUAL STOCK FUNDS

In the 1990s, the top mutual stock funds use "back to basics" as their creed. The mighty Fidelity Magellan Fund ($31.7 billion in assets) focuses on U.S. manufacturing because fund manager Jeff Vinik favors the U.S.'s "low capital costs, a low currency, and low-wages on a worldwide basis. . . ." Another "back to basics" fund is the Dean Witter Dividend Growth Fund. Its manager, Paul Vance, likes stocks over the long term, believing stocks stand to benefit from favorable demographics. Specifically, he sees a much greater portion of our population becoming savers and therefore investors. As far as the long-term economic climate is concerned, Vance sees benign inflation and low long-term interest rates. Given a favorable business investment environment, he favors using the value approach to investing in big-cap companies. Examples of recommended stocks are General Motors, Ford Motor, Minnesota Mining & Manufacturing, and General Electric. Among value stock bargains recommended by other managers for the 25 largest stock funds are banking stocks, particularly the well-situated regional banks, and stocks involved with worker automation such as Hewlett-Packard, Adobe Systems, Analog Devices, and Synoptics Communications.

The relative performance of the 25 largest stock mutual funds varies greatly from fund to fund, measured over the past 5 years. The leaders are 20th Century Ultra Fund and Fidelity Contrafund, recording gains over the past 5 years of 186.25% and 185.82%, respectively. Bringing up the rear are Vanguard Windsor Fund and Vanguard Wellington Fund, registering gains over the past 5 years of only 59.64% and 62.16%, respectively.

Remember, when you select a stock fund you should focus your attention on its relative performance, measured ideally over at least a 5-year period. The biggest mistake usually made in selecting stock funds is to pick the big recent winner for the past year. More often than not the big winner of last year will be the big loser of next year. Usually this briefest of flirtations with success stems from the fact that the fund makes big risky bets that only infrequently pay off.

As testament to the importance of the Fed's first-quarter tightening actions, all of the largest 25 stock mutual funds recorded declines in the first quarter of 1994. Again, there was a fairly wide variation in the size of the first quarter declines among the largest 25 funds. But the bottom line is that Fed policy shifts have an extremely important impact on your investment performance.

DANGER SIGNALS

Unlike bank CDs, your mutual funds are neither insured by the federal government nor necessarily redeemable at par. In short, your mutual funds carry a lot more risk than you may have been led to believe. For an astute investor, this means that you cannot just park your money in a fund and forget about it. You have to keep an eye on the Federal Reserve and significant events in the financial markets. And you have to evaluate the wisdom of your mutual fund's response to these dynamics.

Importantly, most experts believe that a fund's success is directly tied to the skill and expertise of the fund's manager. Since many mutual funds have few investment restraints, you need to take a careful look at the investment practices of your mutual fund manager. Thus, you need to examine the prospectus and quarterly statements of your mutual fund closely and ask your fund manager such questions as:

- What is your money-management experience?
- How long have you managed this fund?
- How much risk will you tolerate?
- How have you diversified the portfolio?
- What is your targeted return?
- What portion of your fund is accounted for by "illiquid" securities including high-yield debt and derivatives?

In addition to these general questions about the nature and performance of the fund, you need to take a close look at any potential return-depressing conflict of interest on the part of the manager. In May 1994, a six-member panel of the Investment Company Institute, the trade association for mutual funds, proposed a voluntary crackdown on personal trading by mutual fund managers. Among the new rules proposed would be a ban on mutual fund managers' purchases of equity in IPOs, severe restrictions on mutual fund managers' purchases of private placements, and restrictions on fund managers' serving on corporate boards. In addition, mutual fund managers must hold a stock bought for their private accounts 60 days before selling it, and preclear all trades with the mutual fund company. Moreover, there should be "blackout days" in which mutual fund managers can't buy or sell a stock for their personal account for seven days after that manager's fund traded in it. Also, all confirmations of personal trades should be sent from the fund manager's brokerage account directly to the fund company compliance office. Furthermore, all mutual fund managers must document once a year all personal securities holdings and sign a statement renewing their commitment to adhere to the rules. It is also at least of some concern that mutual bond funds were investing heavily in junk bonds and other forms of business debt. Indeed, mutual funds have become one of the major suppliers of credit in the high-yield corporate bond market.

You can't help but be impressed by the mutual fund as an investment vehicle. But don't you forget to "kick the tires" before you buy. Remember that the performance of stock and bond funds is closely tied to Fed policy actions. When the Fed is friendly in the form of easy credit, stock and bond funds usually thrive. But when the Fed reverses course and tightens credit, you must take defensive measures.

10

Making Derivatives Work for You (Instead of Against You)

As you seek to take your cue from Fed policy shifts in making timely adjustments in your investment portfolio, you must pay particular attention to a newcomer to the personal investment scene—derivatives. Derivatives are financial instruments whose value is based on, or derived from, other assets such as stocks, bonds, commodities, and foreign currencies.

Most derivatives are of ea plain vanilla type that are used to hedge risks rather than to speculate. These include exchange-listed options and futures and privately traded forwards and swaps. Some mutual fund managers, however, are eager to gain the attractive return from certain exotic derivatives. These derivatives include structured notes securities and mortgage derivatives. The main difficulty is that under volatile financial circumstances these derivatives become highly illiquid and difficult to value. In this regard, the especially volatile global financial market conditions in the spring of 1994 had to give you pause. In particular, we have seen that the Fed's initial February 4, 1994, credit-tightening move led to much greater than expected global financial market volatility. It was almost as though the Fed sneezed, and the German bond market caught pneumonia.

Moreover, in the wake of this Fed credit-tightening step, we saw both the bond and stock markets move downward in tandem. Thus, having a balanced portfolio may not always suffice, in and of itself, to hedge against downside risk. The bottom line is that if you or your mutual funds invest in exotic derivatives, you must be that much more savvy at watching the Fed since interest rate shifts can very quickly do damage to your positions.

In this connection, you should be alerted to the fact that many of the short-term government mutual funds that relied excessively on exotic derivatives to enhance their returns when short-term interest rates were unusually low in 1993 have suffered huge declines in returns and large redemptions in 1994 on the heels of Fed tightening actions and the resulting sudden increase in interest rates. One of these short-term government funds recorded a 15% increase in returns in 1993 when most short-term rates remained around 3%. This was simply too good to be true and, as matters turned out, it was.

UNDERSTANDING DERIVATIVES

Derivatives are financial instruments whose values are linked to the price of some underlying asset. These underlying assets could be virtually anything, but the most popular cash markets to which derivatives are linked are bonds, currencies, stocks, and commodities. The total value of all derivatives is currently estimated at a huge $35 trillion (see Exhibit 10.1). Plain vanilla derivatives come in two basic categories: option-type contracts and forward-type contracts. Options give buyers the potential right but not the obligation to buy or sell an asset at a particular price over a specified period. The option's price is usually a small percentage of the underlying asset's value. Forward-type contracts, which include forwards, futures, and swaps, commit the buyer and seller to trade a given asset at a set price on a future date. By "hedging" tomorrow's transactions at today's prices, a company may not necessarily increase the profit it makes, but it can certainly eliminate much of the risk involved in making it.

Derivatives were created by Wall Street wizards to help clients' businesses (and even individual investors like you) achieve certainty about future costs and revenue streams in an uncertain world. For example, farmers can use agricultural commodity derivatives like futures and options as a way of hedging tomorrow's transactions at today's prices. Specifically, farmers can hedge their corn in the fields and in storage against unforeseen price fluctuations by selling corn futures. Or, as an individual investor, you can

Exhibit 10.1   **Selected Derivatives and Traditional Securities**

Type of Derivative	Current Amount (billions)
Exchange-Traded Derivatives	
Futures	
Interest rate futures	$ 6,400
Stock index futures	150
Currency futures	28
Options	
Interest rate options	3,390
Currency options	390
Stock index options	250
Individual stock options	50
Over-the-Counter Derivatives	
Forwards	
Currency contracts	9,000[1]
Interest rate contracts	3,500[1]
Options	
OTC interest rate options	2,000[1]
OTC currency options	800[1]
Swaps	
Interest rate swaps	8,000[1]
Currency swaps	1,100[1]
Derivatives Securities	
Mortgage derivatives	710
Structured notes	250
Total derivatives (excl. derivatives securities)	35,098
Traditional Securities	
Bonds	18,600
Cash	15,500
Stocks	13,700
Total bonds, cash, stocks	$47,800

[1]Estimates for year-end 1993

Note: The table shows the current breakdown of various derivatives markets, as well as the current outstanding amounts of stocks, bonds, and money market securities worldwide. The numbers are approximate, because totals fluctuate daily and private derivatives are reported inconsistently, if at all.

Source: *The Wall Street Journal,* August 25, 1994. Reprinted by permission of the *Wall Street Journal* © 1994 Dow Jones & Company, Inc. All rights reserved worldwide.

hedge your holdings of foreign stocks and bonds against the risk of unforeseen fluctuations in foreign exchange rates by selling foreign currency futures. (See Chapter 8 for a specific example of how you can hedge your foreign currency risk on foreign investments and precisely how much it would cost.)

Businesses don't always use derivatives to hedge their portfolios. Business managers also can use derivatives to speculate on the future direction of interest rates or commodities prices, which can make a lot of money for the speculator if the view is correct or lose a lot of money if the view is wrong. Many of the more spectacular losses associated with derivatives have come from speculative activities rather than from hedging practices. For instance, the Japanese firm Kashima Oil lost a hefty $1.5 billion trading foreign exchange derivatives, and the German firm Metallgesellschaft, a commodities conglomerate, dropped approximately $1.3 billion trading oil derivatives.

LOOKING AT FUTURES

One type of derivative is a *futures* contract which is an obligation to buy or sell an underlying cash asset at a specified time in the future at a specified price. A futures contract based on either a financial instrument or a financial index is known as a *financial* futures contract. Financial futures can be classified as (1) interest rates futures, (2) stock index futures, or (3) currency futures. The primary exchange-traded interest rate futures contracts include the Treasury 30-year bond futures contract, the municipal bond futures contract, the Eurodollar time deposit futures contract, and the Treasury bill futures contract. Other exchange-traded interest rate futures contracts are based on the 10-year Treasury note, the 5-year Treasury note, and the 2-year Treasury note. Still other types of futures contracts traded on exchanges are based on commodities, foreign exchange, or various equity indices.

It is preferable that, except for specific hedging uses such as against unforeseen foreign currency fluctuations, you should leave speculative futures trading to the professionals. This is because the vast majority of nonprofessional futures traders lose money. To be sure, futures allow you to make big bets on stocks or bonds with little money down. For example, you can buy through a brokerage firm a T-bond contract worth $100,000 for only about $10,000 down. Of course, this allows you to receive the same price gains or losses as someone who actually owns the bond. Thus, you should remember, if you speculate in futures, you could conceivably lose more than your actual investment.

EXERCISING OPTIONS

Another type of derivative is an option, which is *not* an obligation to buy or sell some underlying cash asset at a specified time in the future at a specified price, but rather an *option* to buy or sell. The holder of an option will exercise that option only if a profit is to be made. The profit on an option is the difference between the price the buyer paid for the option and the price received for selling it. This choice must be made before the life of the option runs out, which is usually in a matter of a few months. If the buyer of an option fails to exercise it before it runs out, it will expire worthless and the holder loses the amount paid for it. An option to *buy* is a *call*; an option to *sell* is a *put*. Call options rise in value as the price of the underlying cash asset rises; put options rise in value as price of the underlying cash asset falls.

The best advice is for you to use both options and futures for hedging purposes rather than for speculation. It is true that if you buy an options contract, the most you can lose is the amount you paid for the option. But if you are a seller, or writer, of an option on an asset you don't own—this is called a "naked" option—you are exposed to unlimited losses. Like futures, options allow you to make big bets with little money down on movements in the price of underlying assets.

Both futures and options are traded on regulated exchanges like the Chicago Board of Trade and the Chicago Mercantile Exchange. But other unregulated "over-the-counter" derivatives such as certain types of forwards, options, and swaps are arranged privately between banks, securities companies, corporations, and other big players. These OTC derivatives usually are created to meet the specific needs of a client's portfolio. The largest derivatives dealers include Bankers Trust, Chemical Banking, Citicorp, J. P. Morgan & Co., Merrill Lynch, Morgan Stanley, and Salomon Brothers.

MORTGAGE-BACKED SECURITIES AND THEIR CMO DERIVATIVES

The market for mortgage-backed securities is based on a pool of underlying mortgage loans that generate monthly interest and principal payments that flow through to the ultimate investors. At $1.6 trillion, the mortgage securities market now is more than twice its size as recently as 1987. Three government agencies—the Government National Mortgage Association (Ginnie Mae), the Federal National Mortgage Association (Fannie Mae), and the Federal Home Loan Mortgage Corp (Freddie Mac)—issue most of the pass-through or mortgage-backed securities. These agencies purchase high-quality residential mortgages from bank lenders, package them into mortgage pools, and then sell partial interests in these pools to investors. The most commonly held and traded of all pass-through securities are those representing pools of 30-year maturity, fixed-rate, level-payment mortgages on single-family residential homes. Investors in pass-throughs or mortgage-backed securities receive not only a monthly interest payment but also a partial repayment of principal. (See Exhibit 10.2 for comparison of the basic characteristics of mortgage-backed securities along with U.S. Treasury securities.)

Mortgage-backed bonds can be purchased from any brokerage firm. You have a choice between new issues and other older seasoned issues that are nearer to maturity. For someone in a high tax bracket, seasoned issues may be preferable because the principal repayment component of the old mortgage-backed securities, which is nontaxable, is a much higher percentage of the monthly payout than the interest payment component. In contrast, for newer mortgage-backed issues, the monthly payout consists largely of interest payments that are fully taxable by the federal, state, and local levels of government.

The main shortcoming of mortgage-backed securities is that they don't have a certain maturity date, unlike most fixed-income securities. Each time a mortgage in the pool underlying your mortgage-backed security is retired, you receive your portion of the entire principal of that mortgage in your monthly check. Even more unsettling is the fact that this special repayment risk varies widely with unpredictable swings in interest rates. For example, if interest rates plunge to near-record low levels as they did in the 1991–93

Exhibit 10.2   **Comparison of Selected Features of Mortgage-Backed Securities and U.S. Treasury Securities**

Feature	Mortgage-Backed	Treasuries
Credit risk	General low credit risk	No credit risk
Market risk	Medium to high, depending on degree of general financial market volatility	Low
Liquidity	Fairly good for agency issued mortgage-backed securities	Excellent
Range of maturities	Medium and long-term (fast-paying and older, seasoned pools can provide shorter maturities than stated)	Noncallable (except for certain 30-year bonds)
Frequency of payment	Monthly payments of principal and interest	Semiannual interest payments
Average life	Can only be estimated, owing to prepayment risk	Certain (except for callable bonds)
Basis for yield quotes	Cash flow yield based on monthly payments and a Coupon rate assumption	Based on semiannual coupon payments and a 365-day year

Source: Frank J. Fabozzi, *The Handbook of Fixed Income Securities*, 3rd ed. (Homewood, IL: Business One-Irwin, 1991), p. 576.

period, homeowners will flock to repay their mortgages (see Figure 10.1), and your seasoned mortgage-backed bond will be repaid much earlier than you expected, forcing you to invest the proceeds at unattractively low interest rates. During the 1991–93 period, there were four major waves of mortgage refinancings in late 1991, mid-1992, early 1993, and mid-1993. Just the opposite happens when, as in 1994, the Fed tightens credit abruptly and interest rates shoot up, stopping mortgage prepayments in their tracks. There was a resulting abrupt lengthening in the average maturity of mortgage-backed securities and their collateralized mortgage obligation derivatives as mortgage repayments become less attractive to homeowners in the higher interest rate environment.

In order to try to smooth out the rough spots in mortgage-backed securities caused by erratic repayment patterns, some bright investment bankers created a new type of mortgage derivative security called collateralized mortgage obligations (CMOs). About half the mortgage pass-through securities outstanding have been carved into CMOs. Essentially, a CMO transforms a standard mortgage-

Figure 10.1 **Mortgage Applications for Refinancing, 1991–1994
(March 1990 = 100)**

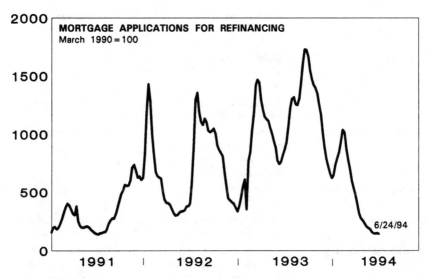

Source: Mortgage Bankers Association.

backed or pass-through security into an array of derivative products. Within each CMO deal, separate tranches are created. Each tranche, in turn, has its own maturity, interest rate, and seniority.

Recent innovations in CMOs have been made to stratify the degree of cash flow variability with respect to changes in prepayments on the underlying collateral. For example, there are planned-amortization-class (PAC) CMOs which are less vulnerable to the risk of mortgage prepayment. In addition, there are interest-only strips (IOs) in which investors receive only the interest portion of mortgage payments, and principal-only strips (POs) in which investors receive only the principal portion of mortgage payments. Also, there are highly risky Z-tranche bonds on which payments are made only after other investors get paid. This process of spreading and compartmentalizing the risk exposure through derivatives has so shielded lenders from the dual risk of rate spikes and prepayment that borrower costs could be reduced significantly. Thus, largely thanks to mortgage derivatives, today's home buyers are paying lower mortgage rates—as much as a full percentage point lower.

The Fed's credit-tightening actions can have a pronounced impact on both mortgage securities and Treasury bonds. This happens because of a curious aspect of mortgage securities. They become more interest-rate sensitive as interest rates rise, and less so as interest rates fall. Of course, this is because more homeowners than expected refinance when rates fall; they stop refinancing when rates rise. As a result, investors who want to maintain a predetermined interest rate sensitivity or duration must buy more Treasury bonds when interest rates are falling and sell more Treasury bonds when interest rates are rising. These investors include insurance companies that have interest-sensitive liabilities, money managers who try to keep pace with a popular fixed-income index, and Wall Street firms.

For an investor in POs, Fed credit-tightening actions that cause homeowners to stop refinancings means waiting longer to get the principal repaid so that these mortgage derivatives plunge in value. In contrast, IOs benefit from rising interest rates, so that these mortgage derivatives rise in value. The opposite happens when the Fed is easing and interest rates are falling. Specifically, mortgage refinancings will skyrocket, adding value to POs, but depressing IOs.

You might reserve a small place in a balanced and well-diversified portfolio for some high-yield fixed-income securities. Among the securities you might include in this section would be corporate junk bonds and mortgage securities. But remember, under certain conditions when there are wide, unforeseen interest-rate swings these securities will quickly come to represent the highly illiquid portion of your fixed-income securities holdings. You can pick up considerable yield on such securities, but don't forget that they all carry high *market risk*. Corporate junk bonds, of course, also carry high *credit risk*, though the credit risk of most mortgage-backed securities is, in contrast, quite low.

USING INTEREST RATE SWAPS

Switching to the borrowing side, corporations may use another form of derivative, interest rate swaps, to try to manage the risks of fluctuating interest rates in a manner that will lower their borrowing costs. Interest rate swaps were invented to help companies easily lock-in fixed borrowing costs when they thought interest rates would rise and slide into floating (variable) borrowing costs when they thought interest rates would fall (see Exhibit 10.3). According to a 1993 study, approximately two-thirds of the 500 largest American companies use derivatives regularly.

Many companies, like homeowners, bet in 1993 that interest rates were nearing their lows and locked-in fixed-rate borrowings. Other companies decided to live more dangerously. They sought to lower interest costs even further by entering into more complex interest rate swap contracts that, in effect, speculated that interest rates would fall further. But the market moved against them. In early February, the Fed tightened its policy and interest rates spiked. Procter & Gamble (P & G) was one company that gambled on interest rates and lost $157 million in the wake of the Fed's shift. Another company, Air Products and Chemicals, announced that it had lost $60 million in a similar gamble on interest rates

Exhibit 10.3   An Interest Rate Swap

WHAT IT IS An agreement between two companies that enables a company that has taken out a floating-rate loan to pay a fixed interest rate.

WHO MIGHT BUY ONE Company A that borrowed money at a floating interest rate, for example the prime plus one percentage point, but is worried that rates might rise.

WHY Company A needs money now but is worried that if interest rates rise it may not be able to afford the higher payments.

THE RISK TO COMPANY A After the swap is set, interest rates may fall but the company would still be obligated to pay the higher fixed rate.

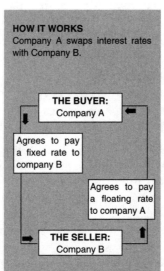

HOW IT WORKS
Company A swaps interest rates with Company B.

THE BUYER:
Company A

Agrees to pay a fixed rate to company B

Agrees to pay a floating rate to company A

THE SELLER:
Company B

WHO WOULD SELL ONE Company B, which is willing to pay floating rates.

WHY Company B believes the floating rate will fall, and it will pay rates that are less than the fixed rate it receives from Company A.

THE RISK TO COMPANY B If rates rise, Company B would end up paying interest rates that are higher than the fixed interest rate it receives from Company A.

WHO WINS? Company A gets the rate it wanted. Company B's success depends on how rates move.

through swaps. Also, Gibson Greeting suffered a similar fate, losing nearly $25 million on interest rate swaps.

WARRANTS, NOTES, AND EXOTIC DERIVATIVES

Even more obscure structured financial products may be used by borrowing companies to do such things as "cap" or limit a company's interest rate cost. These exotic "packages" may include a dozen or more different types of hedges. Essentially, these structured financial products consist of financial instruments with derivatives attached to alter their yield or principal. Because structured financial products are complex borrowing packages, they are usually more difficult to evaluate than straight derivatives. Some of these complex products may entail sizable credit risks involving the party on the other side. Some companies use these structured financings for as much as a third of their borrowings. As a potential investor in these complex and often illiquid structured notes, you should be aware that their interest payments and principal can fluctuate wildly. This is another form of exotic derivative that your money market mutual fund may have invested in to boost returns in 1993 when short-term interest rates were abnormally low. But when interest rates unexpectedly surge higher as they did in the spring of 1994, your mutual fund manager may feel as though these structured note-securities have turned into "toxic waste."

LIQUIDITY IS PARAMOUNT

Regardless of the particular form, all derivatives have one very important thing in common: they are not highly liquid investment vehicles. An asset is liquid if you can convert it into cash quickly and easily without significant loss of principal. During relatively stable financial market conditions, most of the assets in your portfolio will be relatively liquid. Nevertheless, even in normal conditions, Treasury securities are by their nature considerably more liquid than investment-grade corporate bonds, and investment-grade corporate bonds will be more liquid than lower-rated (or unrated) corporate junk bonds or emerging country debt. (Investment-grade corporate bonds are those carrying the four highest ratings: Aaa,

Aa, A, and Baa.) Derivatives are, by their complicated nature, the least liquid of all.

In periods of sharp interest rate swings, it can be expected that Treasury securities will lose a small amount of liquidity and investment-grade corporate debt will lose a *moderate* amount of liquidity. In these same circumstances, unrated corporate junk bonds and emerging country debt will become much more illiquid. And, at the far end of the spectrum, mortgage pass-throughs and mortgage derivatives, such as CMOs, will become *extremely* illiquid, making their daily market valuation difficult, if not impossible.

Bear markets exacerbate the challenge of setting the price for relatively illiquid fixed-income securities. In bearish circumstances, trading volume usually slows to a trickle. With bond trades fewer and smaller in size, firms providing securities pricing services that use real trades as benchmarks find it increasingly difficult to get accurate prices. Mutual funds may receive from these firms providing pricing services distorted daily prices and later are shocked when they try to sell securities and face much lower price bids than expected.

The upshot is that you should closely scrutinize your mutual fund's illiquid investments. Your fund's reliance on exotic derivatives to try to boost its return can be hard on your pocketbook, particularly when interest rates spike higher in the wake of Fed credit-tightening actions.

MAJOR TYPES OF RISK

As an investor, you face two primary kinds of risk, credit risk and market risk. Credit risk, of course, refers to the borrower's ability to repay. All securities have market risk but some, especially exotic derivatives, have more than others. Corporate junk bonds have a lot of credit risk, and Treasury securities have none since they are backed by the full faith and credit of the U.S. government. Mortgage-backed securities generally have low credit risk, but extremely high market risk in certain conditions. This is because of the risk of prepayment that can magnify market risk under conditions of sharp interest-rate fluctuations. For example, on the heels of the Fed's February 4, 1994, tightening move, interest rates shot up, mortgage prepayments plunged, the average maturities of mortgage-backed securities and CMOs lengthened dramatically, and their market risk multiplied.

In the case of emerging-country debt, Mexican high-yield turnpike and freeway authority bonds are examples of debt issues that have both extremely high credit and market risk. This is because they are not backed by the full faith and credit of any governmental unit and are subject to extremely sharp declines in market price (increase in yields) in times of increased economic or political instability.

MANAGING MONEY WITH DERIVATIVES

Aside from deciding whether or not to purchase derivatives for your portfolio, you also need to know to what extent the mutual funds or hedge funds in your portfolio rely on derivatives to increase returns. The Securities and Exchange Commission (SEC), which regulates mutual funds, allows funds to hold as much as 15% of their investments in derivatives and other "illiquid" instruments. Even a smaller than 15% position, however, can wipe out a fund's returns.

David Askin's mutual funds seemed too good to be true, and, as matters turned out, they were. His funds—Granite Partners, Granite Corporation, and Quartz Hedge Fund—promised high yield with low risk. Specifically, Mr. Askin sought to give wealthy individuals and institutions a safe, "market-neutral" place to invest their cash for high returns. Large institutional investors like Marion Merrell Dow, Inc., thought it was a smart move to get a high yield on its idle cash in such a "safe" place.

Borrowing against the $600 million he raised for his funds, Askin pushed the total of his funds up to nearly $2 billion and hedged this principal with IOs and POs. But Askin's hedging techniques incorrectly assumed that these exotic CMOs would enjoy uninterrupted liquidity. Following the Fed's early-1994 tightening action, investors fled the mortgage pass-through and CMO markets. Consequently, these instruments suddenly became illiquid. With interest rates soaring, POs plunged in value and IOs moved up slightly, but not enough to offset collapsing POs. After Askin missed a margin call on his holdings, brokers lending to him seized the securities in his fund portfolios and dumped them on the market, resulting in disastrous consequences for those investing in the Askin funds.

Askin and his investors were not the only ones left holding a bag of worthless derivatives. Other sponsors announcing that their money market or short-term Government income funds have had significant losses in 1994 alone because of investments in derivatives include Piper Jaffrey, Wilmington Trust Corp., BankAmerica, Zweig Fund, Inc., Paine Webber, Kidder Peabody, Fleet, Value Line, Barnett Banks, and CS First Boston Corp. Their experience is an important lesson in the danger derivatives carry for investors: they can expose portfolios to a greater level of market risk and even credit risk. Even so, it does not mean that investors must steer entirely clear of these instruments.

To be sure, as an investor, you will end up taking on more risk by investing in a mutual fund that relies on derivatives to boost its return. But along with greater risk often comes a higher return. For most mutual funds, derivatives account for 2–10% of their asset holdings. What you must do as an investor is monitor your mutual fund manager to be sure that he or she does not rely excessively on derivatives to enhance returns (i.e., more than 10% of its asset holdings), thereby subjecting you to hidden and potentially disastrous risks. Try to determine roughly the extent to which your mutual funds depend on derivative securities to boost returns. And, finally, find out whether those funds that use derivatives have taken a "stress test" to determine how volatile your share prices would be in response to unforeseen shocks like a Fed tightening in credit availability, a dollar crisis, or an outbreak of hostilities like the Gulf War in 1990–91.

USING DERIVATIVES TO BOOST RETURNS

As an investor seeking a reasonable return on your investment holdings, you should minimize reliance on risky CMO derivatives or even more exotic structured notes. To be sure, there may be a small place in your portfolio for high-yield corporate junk bonds, emerging-country debt, and even standard mortgage-backed securities. In any well-diversified investment portfolio, you can, in fact, benefit from the high returns on these high-yield obligations and even on derivatives. But you should always remember that the greater the promised return, the greater the risk. Securitized mortgage derivatives such as IOs and POs offer some of the highest returns available to fixed-income investors, but they also pose prohibitively high risk to your portfolio.

MUTUAL FUNDS USING DERIVATIVES

Your mutual funds' managers may use a wide range of "derivative" securities speculatively in order to swell their returns. But if they guess wrong about the future direction of interest rates and how the derivatives will respond, you stand to lose a lot of principal very quickly. Thus, if you or your mutual fund managers speculate too heavily in derivative securities, you could be asking for bigger headaches than you ever imagined. For example, if you happened to have a portfolio stuffed full of mortgage derivative securities such as CMOs at a time when the Fed embarks on a series of credit-tightening moves, your risk-infested portfolio would have been set up for a significant capital loss. As an individual investor, you should try to minimize reliance on derivatives as investments. If you invest indirectly through mutual funds, ask the sponsor or manager of your mutual funds whether they use derivatives and, if so, to what extent. Your mutual fund owes you a clear description of their strategies, including use of derivatives, and risks inherent in them, as reflected in potential volatility in mutual fund share prices.

In theory, derivatives are here to stay because they can be used in successfully identifying, extracting, and pricing some of the more fundamental risks that drive asset values. But in practice, as an investor, you want to be sure that your mutual funds don't rely excessively on derivatives to boost their return. The proportion of your portfolio accounted for by illiquid securities including derivatives, corporate junk bonds, and emerging-country debt should not exceed 10%.

11

The Four Cardinal Rules
for Savvy Investing

Now that you understand the influence that the Fed holds over the direction of the stock, bond and derivative markets, you are ready to use that influence to your benefit. This chapter will show you how to carefully link your holdings to Fed policy shifts so that you can ride the Fed's coattails in the right direction. In fact, by following four cardinal rules tied to Fed policy actions, you can boost your investment returns and reduce your portfolio risk. The main idea behind this strategy is to allow you to make ongoing adjustments in your investment portfolio so that it keeps in line with the market's cyclical ups and downs. We have found this strategy successful in increasing total returns while at the same time reducing risk, or variability of returns, compared with taking a passive buy-and-hold approach to portfolio management.

THE FOUR CARDINAL RULES
FOR SUCCESSFUL INVESTING

Here are the four rules that sharp-eyed investors use to time and to form their buy, hold, or sell decision:

Rule 1: When the economy slips toward recession, you should wait until the Fed responds with three consecutive easing steps to increase credit availability and to lower short-term interest rates. Then shift your *entire* portfolio into approximately one-half to one-third long-term bonds and one-half to two-thirds stocks. You should take care not to let cash accumulate in your portfolio during these periods. Remember that over long periods of time stocks earn the highest total return (about 10%), cash the lowest (3%), and bonds are in between (roughly 6–7%).

Rule 2: Once the economy finally reverses course and begins to recover, you should continue to hold onto your balanced portfolio so long as inflationary pressures remain dormant and the Fed continues to maintain an accommodative policy stance. The huge bond and stock market rallies in 1993 took place in these conditions.

Rule 3: As the recovery continues to gain momentum, watch closely for early signals of future price pressures, such as a general increase in commodity prices and rising supplier delivery lead times, and related signs, such as stepped-up voluntary business inventory accumulation, increases in prices received by businesses, and increasing credit growth. Wait until the strengthening economy and threats of future price pressures trigger three consecutive Fed steps to tighten the availability of credit and raise short-term interest rates. Then sell all your long-term bonds. Invest half the proceeds from these sales in 2- to 5-year fixed-income securities and half in 3- to 6-month Treasury bills, or 3- to 6-month bank CDs, whichever offers the highest yield. Remember that Treasury bills are not subject to state and local taxes but bank CDs are. One possible alternative to investing in 2- to 5-year Treasury notes might be the Treasury's series EE savings bonds paying a variable yield set at 85% of the average yield on 5-year Treasury notes, with a guaranteed 4% yield minimum, if savings bonds are held for 5 years. Series EE savings bonds are nontransferable, and no more than $15,000 worth of series EE savings bonds can be purchased in the name of any one person in a calendar year. Series EE savings bonds are exempt from state and local taxes, and federal taxes are deferred until redemption.

Rule 4: If the recovery continues to strengthen and inflationary pressures begin to accelerate, you should consider selling up to 25% of your stock holdings and invest the proceeds in some sort of inflation hedge. You might select commodities, real estate, oil, gold, or natural resource funds. All these vehicles would benefit from rising price pressures. Well-diversified natural resources mutual funds with good earnings records include Fidelity Advisor Global Resource, Merrill Lynch Global Resources Trust, and T. Rowe Price New Era Fund.

COMPARING THE JONES PLAN WITH A PASSIVE PORTFOLIO APPROACH

The four cardinal rules for successful investing lie at the heart of the Jones Plan. We've found that this plan enabled us to make timely portfolio adjustments in response to Fed policy shifts. We've also found that this approach improved total returns on stock and bond holdings, relative to a passive portfolio approach in which investors buy and hold. At the same time, it safeguarded principal against unexpectedly sharp interest rate spikes during tight money periods.

Let's take a look at the Jones Plan in action. As can be seen in Figure 11.1, the Jones Plan's investment style begins with a balanced portfolio (in this case, 50% stocks, 50% bonds) and makes two basic switches. In Switch A, following three consecutive Fed moves to tighten or restrain credit availability, you should sell all your long-term 30-year Treasury bonds and invest half the proceeds in short-term 3-month Treasury bills and half in 5-year intermediate-term Treasury notes. Alternatively, in Switch B, following three consecutive Fed moves to ease, or expand, credit availability, you should sell your short-term bills and intermediate-term notes, investing all the proceeds in long-term bonds.

Empirical evidence indicates that if you had followed the Jones Plan during the nearly 25-year period from May 27, 1969, through December 31, 1993, your portfolio would have earned a compound annualized total return of 11.01%, compared with 10.35% in a passive balanced portfolio in which there were no switches. Moreover, if you followed the Jones Plan and made the appropriate portfolio switches in response to Fed policy shifts, your portfolio risk, as measured by the variability of total returns (or

Figure 11.1   Total Returns—Jones Plan Versus Passive Portfolio

Start	Stop	Switch*	Period Returns				Jones Plan		Passive Portfolio	
			Bills	Intermed. Notes	Long Bond	Stocks	Total Weighed Return	Return Value of $1	Total Weighed Return	Return Value of $1
05/27/69	06/23/70	A	7.57%	2.71%	-2.23%	-27.01%	-10.93%	0.890659	-14.62%	0.853800
06/23/70	07/18/72	B	9.63	23.52	31.19	57.68	44.43	1.444340	44.43	1.444340
07/18/72	01/06/75	A	17.51	13.69	4.94	-30.10	-7.25	0.927478	-12.58	0.874187
01/06/75	08/16/77	B	14.98	23.27	29.15	57.94	43.54	1.435423	43.54	1.435423
08/16/77	05/20/80	A	26.70	18.63	-1.81	33.20	27.93	1.279324	15.70	1.156950
05/20/80	11/18/80	B	4.52	-7.14	-9.60	29.40	9.90	1.099013	9.90	1.099013
11/18/80	03/31/81	A	4.71	2.26	1.64	-1.87	0.81	1.008055	-0.12	0.998816
03/31/81	07/13/83	B	28.63	42.74	39.38	34.96	37.17	1.371719	37.17	1.371719
07/13/83	12/18/84	A	13.97	20.58	21.44	9.92	13.60	1.135980	15.68	1.156779
12/18/84	09/13/87	B	18.48	37.95	51.99	121.60	86.80	1.867997	86.80	1.867997
09/13/87	11/04/87	A	1.05	1.54	2.31	-23.25	-10.98	0.890244	-10.47	0.895318
11/04/87	06/22/88	B	4.06	6.27	7.07	11.26	9.16	1.091642	9.16	1.091642
06/22/88	07/27/89	A	8.55	13.38	20.97	31.34	21.15	1.211546	26.16	1.261557
07/27/89	12/31/93	B	25.43	53.35	58.98	55.12	57.05	1.570493	57.05	1.570493
							Jones	13.06497	Passive portfolio	11.27987
25-yr return, annualized	1206.50% 11.01%								25-Yr return, annualized	1027.99% 10.35%
Avg. annual return Standard deviation	23.03% 27.39%								Avg. annual return 21.99% Standard deviation 28.17%	

*Switch A: Following three consecutive Fed-tightening moves, investor should sell long-term bonds and invest half of proceeds in short-term bills and half in intermediate-term 5-year notes. Switch B: Following three consecutive Fed-easing moves, investor should sell short-term bills and intermediate-term 5-year notes and invest proceeds in long-term bonds.
Source: Aubrey G. Lanston & Co., Inc., based on Ibbotson Associates data.

170

standard deviation), would have been less than in the passive port-folio.

To be sure, the Jones Plan works best when there are periods of aggressive Fed-tightening moves. Such was the climate from May 27, 1969, through June 23, 1970, and as you can see in Figure 11.1, during that interval the Jones Plan would have seen a decline of 10.93% in total weighted return while the passive portfolio would have seen a larger decline of 14.62%. Even more striking, during the period from August 16, 1977, through May 20, 1980, under Switch A, the Jones Plan would have produced a 27.93% increase in total weighted return while the increase in the passive portfolio was a much smaller 15.70%.

In contrast, during the decade from July 13, 1983, through December 31, 1993, when price pressures were moderating and Fed-tightening actions were less frequent and less severe, the passive portfolio performed slightly better than the Jones Plan. However, you should be aware that with a string of Fed credit-tightening steps in 1994 and more Fed-tightening actions on the horizon, there is every reason for you to continue following the Jones Plan in the future.

One additional point of interest in Figure 11.1 is worth noting. If you happened to hold *all stocks* in your portfolio instead of the balanced portfolio assumed in the comparison of the Jones Plan and passive portfolio (50% stocks, 50% fixed income), you either had to have a strong stomach for periodic sharp declines in your total returns, or you were in for some sleepless nights. For example, note that during the interval from July 18, 1972, through January 6, 1975, your decline in total return in an equity portfolio would have been 30.10% while in the balanced Jones Plan the decline in total weighted return was 7.25% and for the balanced passive portfolio there was a drop of 12.58%.

INVESTMENT CHOICES WORTH PASSING UP

The Jones Plan has demonstrated that there is strong downside risk to holding only stocks in your portfolio. There are other risks as well that we recommend you avoid. These *don'ts* are aimed at those of you who take a serious interest in your investment portfolio but, at the same time, do not have the time or desire to pursue each of the latest hot stock picks.

Don't make frequent adjustments in your basic investment portfolio. Remember, you are an investor, not a trader.

Don't invest in narrowly focused stock or bond mutual funds unless there is an extremely persuasive argument to do so. Sector stock mutual funds such as health/biotech can be severely depressed by such factors as President Clinton's health care reform proposal. Single state muni bond funds for purposes of avoiding taxes in a particular state are inherently lacking in national diversity, and thus carry significant risk of capital loss. Many of the mutual fund industry's worst performers each year are highly specialized funds, which focus on a sin-gle industry or a particular foreign country or region. Unless you're diversifying your portfolio through multiple, non-related funds, these narrow-casted funds are not recommended.

Don't choose a bond, or bond mutual fund, solely because of its high yield. In the case of high-yield (junk) corporate bonds, remember that if a company is forced to restructure its balance sheet, your debt holdings might suddenly become equity. Such a shift might throw your portfolio off balance and make it a lot more risky than you might have intended. Even worse, some financially weak and politically unstable emerging countries offering high-yield debt obligations might default on their debt. In this case, your investment becomes, in effect, a charitable contribution.

Don't buy mortgage derivative securities, like CMOs, or mutual funds that invest heavily in them (i.e., more than 10% of their assets) unless you are convinced that the interest rate environment will be reasonably stable and mortgage refinancings fairly predictable. In that environment, your derivatives would be at least somewhat liquid and, consequently, less risky. The problem is, of course, that periods when the interest rate environment is reasonably stable and mortgage refinancings are fairly predictable are few and far between.

Don't overlook the possibility of investing directly in fixed-income securities rather than investing indirectly through fixed-income mutual funds. Remember that capital gains realized by your fixed-income mutual funds are taxable. Moreover, your fixed-income mutual funds charge management fees and may have hidden risks if they rely excessively on derivatives to enhance returns.

ADVANCED BOND-INVESTING STRATEGIES

The top bond investors follow specialized bond investment strategies in order to protect themselves from unexpected wholesale losses on their bond holdings. They've found that consistency is the most important ingredient in following any of these strategies. So once you select one of these approaches, remember, above all, stick with it.

Laddering: Instead of buying a single long-term bond, consider a "ladder" of bonds with remaining maturities of, say, 2, 4, 6, 8, and 10 years. Several major "no-load" mutual bond funds offer a wide range of bond maturities.

Duration: Even more than maturity, duration measures a bond's, or bond fund's, sensitivity to interest rate increases or declines. In setting your bond strategy, the idea is to increase the duration of your portfolio when interest rates are steadily declining and, conversely, to shorten the duration of your portfolio when financial market conditions are more volatile and interest rates are spiking higher. You can find out the duration of your bond mutual fund by telephoning the toll-free number of the mutual fund family with which your bond fund is associated and asking the duration of your bond fund. In 1994, when interest rates were spiking higher in volatile conditions, a duration of 2 to 3 years was desirable. In a steadily improving bull market, in contrast, the duration of your bond holdings might be lengthened to as much as 11–12 years. To get a rough idea of the impact that future interest rate changes will have on your bond fund, you merely multiply the fund's duration by the rise or fall in interest rates.

Adjustable-Rate Bond Funds: You might try investing in an adjustable-rate mortgage fund. During the first quarter of 1994, adjustable-rate mortgage funds were one of the few types of bond funds that did not show a negative total return. To be sure, the total first-quarter return for adjustable-rate mortgage funds rose only 0.06%. Nevertheless, it looked good compared with a decline of 2.79% in the total return for fixed-rate U.S. mortgage funds during the same period.

The best thing to keep in mind about your specialized bond-investing strategies is that they are intended to protect your portfolio from unpleasant surprises. The idea is to follow consistent strategies that protect your portfolio from outside shocks like wars or oil price spurts or inside shocks like Fed credit-tightening actions.

TAKING A LONG VIEW

As an investor who made a lot of money in stock and bond mutual funds in 1993, you would do well to stand back and take a look at the longer-term picture. The past decade has seen, with the exception of the sharp but brief crash in 1987, and a smaller collapse in 1989, a spectacular, decade-long stock market rally. The S&P 500 stock index has soared nearly fivefold to a peak of just under 480 at the end of January 1994 from 100 in August 1982 (see Figure 11.2). Similarly, the bond market has also staged a powerful rally during the past decade or so as 30-year Treasury bond yields have fallen to a low of 5.78% in October 1993 from a peak of over 15% in 1981.

Following the immutable law of the financial jungle, the high-flying stock and bond markets are likely to face a "regression to the mean" in the 1990s. In other words, what goes up must come down. Financial assets like stocks and bonds over-performed during the past decade and odds are they will underperform in the current decade. As global economic growth strengthens in coming years and price pressures reawaken, the long-dormant prices of real assets such as timber, oil, gold, and real estate could perk up. In the meantime, liquid, short-term assets (especially 3- to 6-month Treasury bills) are a good resting spot or stopping-off point as the Fed moves to curtail the availability of credit and boost short-term interest rates.

Your best bet as an individual investor may be to invest di-

Figure 11.2 **S&P 500 Index and the 30-Year Bond Yield, 1977–1994**

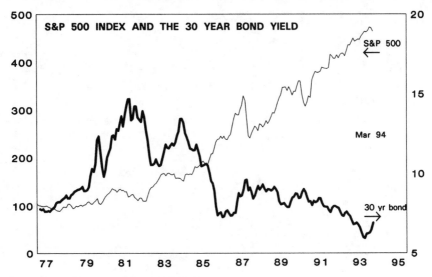

Source: Federal Reserve and Standard & Poor's.

rectly in 3- to 6-month Treasury bills as your major short-term holdings, rather than investing indirectly through money market mutual funds. Money market mutual funds are less attractive in that they charge a management fee and they may have a hidden, excessive reliance on derivatives. Whether you choose short-term Treasury bills or bank CDs as your primary short-term asset holdings should depend on which pays the highest yield. Remember also that Treasury bills are exempt from state and local taxes, while bank CDs are not.

12

How the Federal Reserve Can
Make Your Financial Future

So far, we have seen a dependable pathway through the financial jungle to investment success. Now we will look at how you can use this path in the coming years and perpetuate your stronger returns. Throughout your journey, you will find that the economy and the Federal Reserve's actions will be the beacons guiding your most sound and profitable investment choices.

INVESTORS WILL DRIVE ELECTION RESULTS

With 30% of all U.S. households now holding some type of mutual fund, and the consequential heightened sensitivity of voters to stock and bond price fluctuations, politicians will begin to pay more attention to the fortunes of the financial markets. In fact, when the 1996 presidential election year comes around, it is likely that you and your fellow investors will exert an important influence on the election outcome. In short, the fate of the stock market is likely to carry considerable weight in the election results.

Taking a broader perspective, you and your fellow investors have played a part in a major economic and political event. You have been instrumental in closing the age-old "gap" between "Wall Street" and "Main Street." In the past, populist politicians used to rail endlessly about the wide gulf between the big, evil, monied interests on "Wall Street" and the small, virtuous, hard-working folks on "Main Street."

Today, with a mounting number of "Main Street" households holding globally diversified investment portfolios, they have a growing identification with "Wall Street." Everyone, including the big, bad "Wall Street" interests and the small, God-fearing people on "Main Street" now have coinciding interests in good stock and bond market performances. With their constituents so deeply concerned with developments on "Wall Street," there is likely to be a growing preoccupation of the president and most other politicians with developments in the stock and bond markets. In turn, this democratization of "Wall Street" is likely to have an important and lasting impact on relations between the government and the Fed. In the final analysis, it is the believability of the Fed's words and actions that usually has the most direct bearing on bond and stock market fortunes.

A NEW TWIST IN GOVERNMENT-FED RELATIONS

President Bill Clinton's courting of Fed Chairman Alan Greenspan to lend credibility to his economic program may have set a precedent for future presidents. In turn, the current Fed chairman, who is highly respected by large and small investors alike, has instilled in the president the need to work on the fiscal side for lower deficits in order to achieve bond market credibility. In the future, the first order of business for succeeding presidents will be to design economic and budget programs that calm the fears of bond investors concerning lingering threats of out-of-control deficits and future runaway inflation.

The upshot of these important developments is that there will be greater pressure for future administrations to create a stronger relationship with the Fed. The purpose of this effort will be to achieve greater credibility in the global financial markets.

First and foremost, future administrations will be playing to a gallery of domestic *and* foreign investors who are moving a huge pool of mobile capital around the world in search of the countries that produce the political and economic conditions that generate the highest relative real returns. In some ways, this is a global referendum on the performance of the governments of the United States and other countries which compete for this huge pool of mobile capital to finance their private and public investment needs. A weak administration with poor control over budget deficits and uncertain inflation prospects will lose ground in this wide open competition for the pool of global capital, managed for the most part by return-conscious institutional investors like mutual funds, hedge funds, and pension funds.

As an individual investor, you should benefit from this new "financial world order." The resulting disciplined political and economic environment should be conducive to future steady and solid growth in the returns on your investment portfolio. Future administrations will realize that they must follow generally constrained budget policies that seek to reduce deficits, while at the same time giving independent central banks like the Fed the leeway to pursue longer-term price stability. Of course, this is not the stuff of which speculative stock and bond market rallies are made. Accordingly, it lessens the opportunity for you to make a quick killing on your stock and bond investments. Just the same, in the future you should be able to count on your investments growing in an orderly and fairly predictable manner with tolerable risk, as you seek to achieve your ultimate goal of financial independence.

IMPORTANT FED-WATCHING TIPS

When you are seeking to anticipate Fed-tightening actions, remember above all to watch the same indicators of future price pressures that the Fed is watching. In the past, the Fed used the money supply as its primary and most reliable indicator of future price pressures. Because of deregulation, securitization, globalization, and the development of new financial products, it is no longer possible to rely on a single indicator like the money supply in formulating monetary policy. Instead, the Fed is currently watching as signals of future price pressures a variety of factors such as a general increase in commodity prices. Fed officials are also looking for rising supplier delivery lead times and related signs of stepped-up deliberate business inventory accumulation, especially if this process leads to increases in prices paid and received by businesses. In addition, the monetary authorities are watching for increasing credit growth, as both bank and nonbank lenders and investors meet the demands of individuals and businesses in an expanding economy.

As the economy reaches the advanced stages of recovery, you

should keep an eye open for signs of increasing pressures on productive resources. Such conditions will cause the monetary authorities to err on the side of restraint and higher interest rates. Conversely, if economic activity is weakening, unemployment is rising and inflationary pressures are declining, the monetary authorities are likely to err on the side of easing credit and pushing interest rates lower.

PARTICIPATING IN A RAPIDLY EVOLVING GLOBAL INTERMEDIATION PROCESS

With the net assets of mutual funds rising above $2 trillion in 1993, you and your fellow mutual fund investors are now participating in a new and massive global intermediation process. It involves the pooling of savings and their channeling into profitable debt and equity investments around the world. As individual investors involved in this global intermediation process, you face the prospect of higher returns but with higher risk. This global intermediation process has allocated credit more efficiently through the capital markets. In addition, new financial innovations like derivatives spread lender risk over time and across continents, thereby allowing lenders to share their risk with others and reducing the cost of borrowing for individuals and businesses below what it otherwise would have been. These forces have a stimulating effect on global economic activity.

Currently, overregulated banks, the traditional medium for intermediation, have turned increasingly to fee-based activities such as securitization, providing investment advice, securities custody, and processing services. Banks have even begun to market their own mutual funds to their depositors. In addition, large global bankers have turned for profits to increased proprietary securities and currency trading and to the development of derivatives like interest rate and currency swaps.

Since banks have traditionally been the primary point of contact for monetary policy, Fed officials must take into account the diminished share of banks in the total supply of credit. In the future, the Fed will probably find it more difficult to determine just how forceful it should be in either tightening credit (or easing it), in order to have the same impact on economic activity as in the past when banks supplied a bigger share of total credit.

Importantly, the pool of savings managed by professionals is growing rapidly as private pension plans supplement public ones, and as savings shift from the banking sector to mutual funds. As a result, the pooling of savings and their intermediation into high-return investments will increasingly become a global effort. In contrast, the pattern in the past has been one in which domestic savings largely flowed into domestic investment opportunities within individual countries.

In this new world, rapid global shifts of huge pools of mobile, liquid capital and information may serve to discipline national economic policy measures. If, for example, any developed or emerging country tries to boost growth to an excessive and potentially inflationary pace for political reasons, global institutional investors will become fearful of the increased inflationary threat and sell its bonds, thus pushing long-term interest rates higher and choking off growth. Accordingly, the best any major country can do for its citizens is to create a favorable economic climate for participation in the world economy. This favorable climate should consist primarily of productivity-enhancing measures such as keeping inflation low, investing heavily in education and job training, promoting research and development, rewarding savings and investment, and penalizing consumption. In these circumstances, Fed anti-inflation credibility and consistency are of crucial importance.

MIND-BOGGLING FUTURISTIC FINANCIAL TRENDS

The future promises still more financial product innovation to facilitate the global intermediation process. Significantly, international diversification is still in its adolescence. The costs of gathering, processing, and transmitting information and executing financial transactions will almost certainly decline further with advances in technology.

The United States is likely to continue in the forefront of the revolution in personal finance. Importantly, some of our best scientific minds are at work in developing and trading financial derivatives. Derivatives play a key role in the formation of capital and the management of risk, helping producers of goods and services borrow at lower interest costs than otherwise would have been the case and delivering the best goods and services at the lowest cost. Applying futuristic principles of "particle finance," credit risks will be desegregated into discrete attributes that will be readily traded, unbundled, and rebundled. In the future, intermediaries will make markets in credit risk attributes and in bundles of attributes customized to suit the particular needs of their clients.

"Particle finance," combined with more powerful technology, will allow you and your fellow investors to quantify, price, and manage today's familiar risks. Conceivably, it might even be possible to uncover, quantify, price, and manage risks that exist today but are hidden from view. Among the practical applications of this effort today might be that of limiting an airline's exposure to future fuel price increases or helping a company hedge the value of a pending acquisition.

From the standpoint of your investment portfolio, "particle finance" and automated analytics would provide much better asset allocation advice than is available today. You might be able to allocate your investment holdings across many financial attributes rather than just picking the appropriate stock-bond balance.

In the future, financial specialists in particle finance will provide you with a creative grasp of new financial possibilities. They will also help you understand the true nature of risk and return. Investments in underlying securities such as stocks and bonds represent an indivisible conglomeration of market risks—you are either long 20 bonds or short 20 bonds, and you have no way of isolating the risks associated with volatility or the passage of time. Derivatives allow you to isolate these risks and approach them individually—the "divide and conquer" approach to managing risk. You will have the opportunity, and the challenge, of deciphering a bewildering alphabet of financial risks.

> **Delta risk**—price risk, or how price changes affect your portfolio value
>
> **Gamma risk**—how price risk changes as time passes and as price levels change
>
> **Vega risk**—volatility risk, or how portfolio value varies with implied volatility

Theta risk—time risk, or how portfolio value changes as "time value" is used up

"Delta," or price risk, describes how portfolio value varies with underlying market prices—it is simply a number that tells you how long or short your portfolio is. For a simple stock or bond investment, delta risk is constant for the life of the position. A portfolio including derivatives, however, has a *dynamic delta*, because risks are further divided and identified. "Gamma" risk describes how delta changes as time passes and as price levels change. "Vega" risk describes how portfolio value varies with the implied volatility of the underlying markets. And "theta" risk describes how portfolio value varies as the "time value" of derivative instruments is used up. Derivatives give you the flexibility of building positions whose exposure to the market changes over time according to your assessment of future risks and rewards.

Looking ahead, your personal investment options are likely to be virtually limitless. Your potential returns are higher than in the past, but so are your risks. With added risks in your portfolio, you simply must assume greater responsibility for managing these risks and for keeping tabs on the Fed and the other major economic influences on your investment performance. This is true regardless of whether you invest directly in stocks, bonds, and other assets or through mutual funds.

Bibliography

Books

Changing Capital Markets: Implications for Monetary Policy, A Symposium Sponsored by the Federal Reserve Bank of Kansas City, Jackson Hole, Wyoming, August 19–21, 1993.

Colander, David C. and Daane, Dewey, *The Art of Monetary Policy* (Armonk, N.Y.: M.E. Sharpe, 1994).

Fabozzi, Frank J., *The Handbook of Fixed Income Securities*, 3rd Edition (Homewood, Ill.: Business One Irwin, 1991).

Greider, William, *Secrets of the Temple: How the Federal Reserve Runs the Country* (New York, N.Y.: Simon & Schuster, 1987).

Henderson, John and Scott, Jonathan P., *Securitization* (New York, N.Y.: NYIF/Simon & Schuster, 1988).

Jones, David M., *Fed Watching and Interest Rate Projections: A Practical Guide*, 2nd Edition (New York, N.Y.: NYIF/Simon and Schuster, 1989).

——, *The Politics of Money: The Fed Under Alan Greenspan* (New York, N.Y.: NYIF/Simon & Schuster, 1991).

Kavros, Harry, *First Boston's Desktop Guide to the Fixed Income Securities Market* (Chicago, Ill.: Probus Publishing Company, 1989).

Kettl, Donald F., *Leadership at the Fed* (New Haven, Conn.: Yale University Press, 1986).

Lynch, Peter, *Beating the Street* (New York, N.Y.: Simon & Schuster, 1993).

Mennis, Edmund A., *How the Economy Works* (New York, N.Y.: NYIF/Simon & Schuster, 1991).

Meulendyke, Ann-Marie, *U.S. Monetary Policy and Financial Markets* (New York, N.Y.: Federal Reserve Bank of New York, 1989).

Natenberg, Sheldon, *Option Volatility and Pricing Strategies* (Chicago, Ill..: Probus Publishing Company, 1988).

Prestbo, John and Sease, Douglas, *Barron's Guide to Making Investment Decisions* (Englewood Cliffs, N.J.: Prentice Hall, 1994).

The Federal Reserve System: Purposes and Functions, 7th Edition (Washington, D.C.: Board of Governors of the Federal Reserve, 1984).

Woodward, Bob, *The Agenda: Inside the Clinton White House* (New York, N.Y.: Simon & Schuster, 1994).

Articles, Research Papers, and Congressional Testimony

Akhtar, M. A. and Howe, Howard, "The Political and Institutional Independence of U.S. Monetary Policy," Bank Nazionale de Lavoro, *Quarterly Review* No. 178 (September, 1991).

Asinof, Lynn, "How to Keep Your Balance in Uncertain Markets," *Wall Street Journal* (February 28, 1994).

Bernanke, Ben S., "Credit in the Macroeconomy," *Quarterly Review*, Federal Reserve Bank of New York (Spring, 1993).

Cantor, Richard and Wenninger, John, "Perspective on the Credit Slowdown," *Quarterly Review*, Federal Reserve Bank of New York (Spring, 1993).

Clements, Jonathan, "Beware of Portfolio Risks as You Seek Rewards," *Wall Street Journal* (April 9, 1994).

——, "Ten Questions Mutual-Fund Investors Should Ask," *Wall Street Journal* (January 14, 1994).

Cross, Sam T., "Following the Bundesbank: The Spread of Central Bank Independence," *Foreign Affairs* (March/April 1994).

Davis, Richard G. (ed.), "Intermediate Targets and Indicators for

Monetary Policy: A Critical Survey," (New York, N.Y.: Federal Reserve Bank of New York, 1990).

Dorfman, John R., "Why Panic When You Can Buy? Key Managers See Upside," *Wall Street Journal* (April 7, 1994).

Drucker, Peter F., "Trade Lessons from the World Economy," *Foreign Affairs* (January/February, 1994).

Fernald, Julia, Keane, Frank and **Mosser, Patricia C.,** "Mortgage Security Hedging and the Yield Curve," Research Paper #9411 (New York, N.Y.: Federal Reserve Bank of New York, 1994).

Gottschalk Jr., Earl C., "Avoiding the Big Mistakes Along Life's Path," *Wall Street Journal* (May 27, 1994).

Gould, Carole, "Facing the Currency Risk Question," *New York Times* (September 4, 1994).

Granito, Donnelly Barbara, "Global Diversification Has Its Downside and May Not Be the Strongest Safety Net," *Wall Street Journal* (April 13, 1994).

Greenspan, Alan, "FDICIA and the Future of Banking Law and Regulation," Remarks to the 29th Annual Conference on Bank Structure and Competition, Chicago, Illinois (May 6, 1993).

——, testimony before the Committee on Banking, Housing and Urban Affairs, United States Senate (February 19, 1993).

——, testimony before the Committee on Banking, Housing and Urban Affairs, United States Senate (July 22, 1993).

——, testimony before the Joint Economic Committee, U.S. Congress (January 31, 1994).

Hale, David, "The Economic Consequences of America's Mutual Fund Boom," *The International Economy* (March/April, 1994).

Hansell, Saul, "A Bad Bet for P & G," *New York Times* (April 14, 1994).

Henriques, Diana B., "Questions of Conflict Sting Mutual Funds," *New York Times* (August 7, 1994).

Jereski, Laura, "Mortgage Securities Weaken Fed's Power," *Wall Street Journal* (August 30, 1994).

——, and **Vogel Jr., Thomas T.,** "Assessing Bond Values Gets Harder," *Wall Street Journal* (June 13, 1994).

Jones, David M., "The Role of Credit in Economic Activity," *Quarterly Review*, Federal Reserve Bank of New York (Spring, 1993).

Lipin, Steven, "Bankers Trust Sued on Derivatives," *Wall Street Journal* (September 13, 1994).

Mack, Phillip R., "Recent Trends in the Mutual Fund Industry," *Federal Reserve Bulletin* (November, 1993).

McGough, Robert, "Mutual Misery: Funds Slide," *Wall Street Journal* (July 7, 1994).

McNees, Stephen K., "The Discount Rate: The Other Tool of Monetary Policy," *New England Economic Review*, Federal Reserve Bank of Boston (July/August, 1993).

Morgan, Donald P., "Asymmetric Effects of Monetary Policy," *Economic Review*, Federal Reserve Bank of Kansas City (Second Quarter, 1993).

Muehring, Kevin, "Grasping Greenspanomics," *Institutional Investor* (June, 1993).

Norris, Floyd, "S&P, Responding to Its Rival, Introduces a New Stock Index," *New York Times*, (October 18, 1994).

Sesit, Michael R., "Americans Pour Money Into Foreign Markets," *Wall Street Journal* (April 13, 1994).

Stocks, Bonds, Bills and Inflation, 1994 Yearbook (Chicago, Illinois: Ibbotsen Associates, 1994).

INDEX